An **ART WORLD EXPLORER** *guide*

VENICE
2023
ARCHITECTURE
BIENNALE
LISTINGS - PLANNER - MAP

D1725090

By Vici MacDonald

An ART WORLD EXPLORER guide

PUBLISHED IN 2023 BY REVERSE PRESS | ISBN 978-1-910991-12-1 | IMPRESSION 1

Venice's symbol, a winged lion, on
its pillar in Piazza San Marco
Photo © Vici MacDonald

An independent guide to Venice's 2023 Architecture Biennale season

YOUR ONE-STOP VISIT PLANNER

The 18th Venice Architecture Biennale, titled 'The Laboratory of the Future', runs from 20 May to 26 November 2023. It has many strands, with pavilions and collateral events throughout the city. This book offers a well-organized listings guide to the event, with handy breakdowns of what to see where. The useful information inside includes maps, descriptions, times, prices, tips, photos, and index. It's an invaluable resource for anyone planning a visit.

ABOUT THE AUTHOR

Vici MacDonald is a former editor of contemporary art magazine *Art World*, and has contributed design and editorial to periodicals including *The Art Newspaper* and *Tate* magazine. She has art directed specialist publications for major art world events such as Art Basel and Frieze, and created guides to several previous Venice Art Biennales.

Visitors flocking to the 2023 Architecture Biennale
Photo by Jacopo Salvi. Courtesy La Biennale di Venezia

CONTENTS

There's a lot more to Venice than the Bridge of Sighs
Photo © Vici MacDonald

USING THIS GUIDE

If there's one event that showcases the architecture world like no other, it's the Venice Architecture Biennale, inaugurated in 1980 and still going strong. In 2023 – a year out of step, due to the Covid pandemic – it presents its 18th edition, titled 'The Laboratory of the Future'.

It offers a huge amount to see, with several elements. As well as ticketed exhibitions in the Giardini and Arsenale, there are free-to-enter pavilions throughout the city, plus a separate strand called Collateral Events.

With so much on, it can be difficult to get a handle on it all – hence this guide. The book is divided into the following sections:

INFORMATION

A brief guide to getting started with the Biennale, including the ticket types available and how to buy them, descriptions of the exhibition areas, plus dates, times, and other practical details. The information continues at the end of the book, with an index of exhibitions, and an index of addresses.

MAPS

The maps show every Biennale exhibition and event venue listed, plus all the vaporetto (waterbus) stops, so you can easily see what else is nearby. There is a map of all the venues in Venice city, plus close-up maps of the Arsenale and Giardini areas. The numbers on the maps cross-refer to the listings (see below). These give full street addresses, and can be used with an online map to get accurate location info.

LISTINGS

The listings are broken up into three sections, each with its own contents list. Exhibitions and events are arranged in alphabetical order within their section. Each has its own page, with all the info you could need. The sections are:

➲ **THE LABORATORY OF THE FUTURE:** An overview of the Biennale's central exhibition, split between the Giardini and the Arsenale. There's also an offsite project in mainland Mestre. This section explains the curatorial strands, and includes detailed exhibition plans, plus A-Z lists of the participants' locations and biographies.

➲ **NATIONAL PAVILIONS:** Exhibitions by countries invited to participate in the official Biennale. They are spread out through the Giardini, the Arsenale, Venice city, and nearby San Servolo. Also included this year is a 'special pavilion' by the V&A Museum.

➲ **COLLATERAL EVENTS:** Official Biennale exhibitions by non-profit institutions, plus regions such as Scotland and Catalonia. All are free, and all are held in Venice city.

A NOTE FROM THE AUTHOR

Thank you for buying this book, and I hope you find it helpful. All the listings have been researched from primary sources – exhibitors, institutions, venues, and Biennale literature – and not from a trawl of other lists. It's all as accurate as possible at time of press in May 2023, just after the Biennale's start.

The book size was chosen to be as portable as possible, while fitting in all the necessary information. The black-and-white printing was necessary to make it affordable. Its usefulness will hopefully outshine the humble production quality.

Content-wise, each exhibition or event gets its own page, with all the facts in one place – address, times, prices, visitor tips and so on. The map section is not intended as a street guide, but rather as a handy reference for seeing which venues are close to each other, and their nearest boat stops.

I hope you enjoy the plethora of inspiring architecture in this wonderful city as much as I do – and that this little book helps you to see as much of it as possible.

Vici MacDonald

The Biennale's two main sites, the Giardini (above) and the Arsenale (below)
Photos by Francesco Galli (Giardini) and Andrea Avezzù (Arsenale). Courtesy La Biennale di Venezia

BIENNALE BASICS

The Venice Biennale has two main exhibition sites, the Giardini and the Arsenale. These require a ticket for entry – one ticket gives access to both places. There are also many Biennale shows held in temporary venues throughout Venice city. These are usually free to enter, with no ticket required.

THE GIARDINI

The permanent national pavilions in the Giardini della Biennale are what distinguish Venice from other such biennales. Developed from 1907 onwards, these buildings offer a fascinating collage of architectural styles, from Hungary's ornate mosaics to Switzerland's refined modernism. They also reflect the tides of geopolitics, with some bearing now-defunct names such as Yugoslavia (which is set in stone, so there's now an extra sign by the door saying 'Serbia').

THE ARSENALE

This ancient military and naval complex takes up a sixth of Venice's total area, and is usually closed to the public – but during the Biennale, its magnificent grounds are open to all. There's much to explore, including the famous Corderie (an immensely long ex-ropemaking works), the arcaded shipyards of Gaggiandre, acres of brick warehouses, and a historic 19th-century crane. Photo opportunities abound, and its peaceful backwaters feel a world away from the general Venetian frenzy.

VENICE CITY

Many Biennale shows spill out into Venice city itself, occupying a host of fascinating buildings, such as grand palazzi, places of worship, municipal buildings, and defunct shops. Visiting such venues is an experience in itself, and takes you to parts of the island – and other nearby islands – that most tourists never reach.

BUYING TICKETS

Given the amount there is to see, Biennale ticket prices are very reasonable. There are various options available, and if staying for several days, consider one that allows multiple entry. You can then freely come and go between Venice city and the Arsenale and Giardini – for instance to visit a restaurant for lunch. Tickets can be bought online only – it's fairly easy to do, and there are help desks at the gates. See the Biennale's website (below) for details.

BIENNALE WEBSITE

There's a huge amount of info on the Biennale website, but it's a bit confusing to navigate. Here are three links for getting started.

- ➲ **HOME PAGE:** *labiennale.org/en/architecture/2023*
- ➲ **GENERAL INFO:** *labiennale.org/en/architecture/2023/information*
- ➲ **NATIONAL PAVILIONS:** *labiennale.org/en/architecture/2023/national-participations*

VISITING

DATES: 20 May–26 Nov 2023

GIARDINI HOURS:
20 May–30 Sep:
Tue–Sun 11:00–19:00
1 Oct–26 Nov:
Tue–Sun 10:00–18:00
Last entry 15 mins before closing

ARSENALE HOURS: As Giardini, except 20 May–30 Sep there is late opening on Fri and Sat until 20:00

FORTE MARGHERA HOURS:
Tue–Sun 12:00–20:00

CLOSED: Mon (except 22 May, 14 Aug, 4 Sep, 16 Oct, 30 Oct, 20 Nov)

ADMISSION: Biennale ticket. Available online only. See below for further details. Mestre is free

TICKET INFO: labiennale. org/en/architecture/2023/ information#tickets

TICKET SALES: labiennale.vivaticket.it

TICKET PRICES

Single entry ticket

Valid for one entry to the Giardini and one entry to the Arsenale. These can be on different days.

FULL: € 25
CONCESSIONS: Over 65: €20
Students and/or under 26: €16

Multiple access ticket

Allows multiple re-entry for 3 or 7 consecutive days from first entry (closing days excluded).

3 DAYS: €35
7 DAYS: €45
CONCESSIONS: None

Accreditation

Allows re-entry for the entire Biennale (closing days excluded).

FULL: €75
CONCESSIONS: Students and/or under 26: €45

➲ *Note that photo ID (such as a passport) is required at the entrance for concessions, multiple access tickets, and accreditations. Children under six get free entry to everything, upon proof of age*

The city seen from St Mark's campanile – there's plenty to explore
Photo © Vici MacDonald

MAPS

An overview of what's where

The maps show every venue listed, plus all the vaporetto (waterbus) stops, so you can easily see what else is nearby. The numbers on the maps cross-refer to the listings pages. These give full street addresses, which can be used with an online map to get accurate location info.

SECTION CONTENTS

GIARDINI AREA MAP

See p. 26 for Giardini 'The Laboratory of the Future' exhibition plan

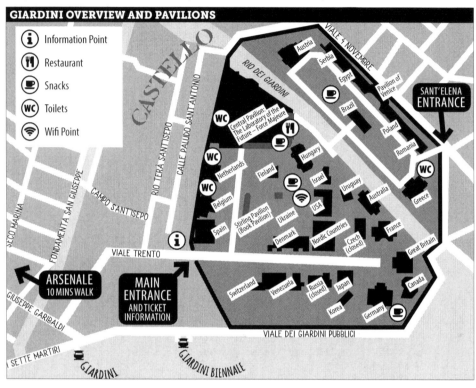

GIARDINI OVERVIEW AND PAVILIONS

- (i) Information Point
- (🍴) Restaurant
- (☕) Snacks
- (WC) Toilets
- (📶) Wifi Point

SANT'ELENA ENTRANCE

ARSENALE 10 MINS WALK

MAIN ENTRANCE AND TICKET INFORMATION

VIALE TRENTO

VIALE DEI GIARDINI PUBBLICI

Giardini Pavilions

See above for locations

COUNTRY	CODE
Australia	AU
Austria	AT
Belgium	BE
Brazil	BR
Canada	CA
Denmark	DK
Egypt	EG
Finland	FI
France	FR
Germany	DE
Great Britain	GB
Greece	GR
Hungary	HU
Israel	IL
Japan	JP
Korea (Republic of)	KR
Netherlands (The)	NL

COUNTRY	CODE
Nordic Countries (Finland, Norway, Sweden)	PN
Poland	PL
Romania	RO
Serbia	RS
Spain	ES
Switzerland	CH
Ukraine	UA
United States of America	US
Uruguay	UY
Venezuela (Bolivarian Republic of)	VE

SPECIAL PAVILIONS

Central Pavilion	
Pavilion of Venice	PVE

Arsenale Pavilions

See right for locations

COUNTRY	CODE
Albania	AL
Argentina	AR
Bahrain (Kingdom of)	BH
Chile	CL
China (People's Republic of)	CN
Croatia	HR
Czech Republic	CZ
Grand Duchy of Luxembourg	LU
Ireland	IE
Italy	ITALIA
Latvia	LV
Mexico	MX
Peru	PE
Philippines	PH
Republic of Kosovo	KS
Saudi Arabia	SA
Singapore	SG
Slovenia (Republic of)	SI

COUNTRY	CODE
South Africa (Republic of)	ZA
Türkiye (Turkey)	TR
Ukraine	UA
United Arab Emirates	AE
Uzbekistan (Republic of)	UZ

SPECIAL PAVILIONS

Applied Arts Pavilion (V & A Museum)	PAA

Country codes

These are the official Biennale acronyms for the various pavilions, used throughout all the Biennale literature and signage

ARSENALE AREA MAP

See p. 28 for Arsenale 'The Laboratory of the Future' exhibition plan

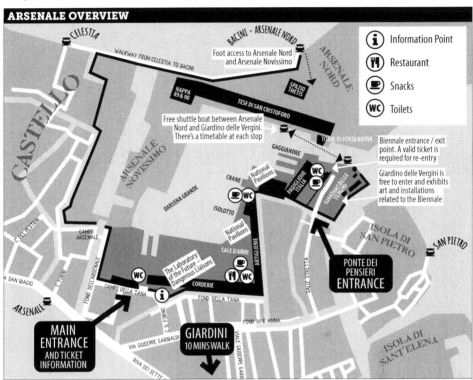

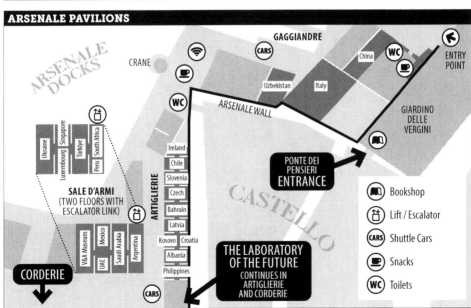

VENICE CITY VENUE MAP

See exhibition listings section starting p.16 for full details of each venue

MESTRE

SANT'ALVISE

ORTO

L/1 Forte Marghera –
Sweet Water Foundation
(see p. 29 for map)

TRE ARCHI

CANNAREGIO

CALLE

CAMPO
GHETTO
NUOVO

N/14 Romania
(also in Giardini)

GUGLIE

SAN MARCUOLA

CAMPO
SAN
SEREMA

FONDAMEN

RAILWAY
STATION

RIVA DI BIASIO

SAN STAE

C/5 EUmies Awards

C/9 Tracé Bleu

FERROVIA

C/6 Radical Yet
Possible (25 May)

C/7 Radical Yet
Possible (26 May)

CAMPO SAN
GIACOMO
DALL'ORIO

CA' D'ORO

RIALTO MERCATO

CAMPO SAN
GIOVANNI
E PAOLO

CAR PARKS

PIAZZALE ROMA

C/3 Climate
Wunderkammer

SAN POLO

RIALTO
MARKET

RIALTO

CAMPO
SAN
STIN

CAMPO
SAN
POLO

CAMPO
SAN
SILVESTRO

CAMPO
SANTA MARIA
FORMOSA

PIAZZALE
ROMA

CAMPO
DEI
TOLENTINI

SANTA CROCE

CAMPO
DEI
FRARI

SAN SILVESTRO

N/11 North Macedonia

SANT' ANGELO

SANTA MARTA

C/8 Students As Researchers

CAMPO
SANTA
MARGHERITA

SAN TOMA

SAN SAMUELE

CAMPO
SANT'
ANGELO

CAMPO
MANIN

PIAZZA
SAN MARCO

CAMPO SAN
BARNABA

CA' REZZONICO

ACCADEMIA

CAMPO SAN
STEFANO

CAMPO SAN
MAURIZIO

SAN MARCO

SAN MARCO GIARDINETTI

DORSODURO

CAMPO DE
S. ANZOLO
E FELXE

N/13 Portugal

GIGLIO

SALUTE

SAN MARCO VALLARESSO

CAMPO
DELLA
SALUTE

SAN BASILIO

SAN G

SACCA FISOLA

MOLINO STUCKY

N/1 Bulgaria

N/9 Montenegro

N/7 Kuwait

SACCA FISOLA

ZATTERE

SPIRITO SANTO

ZITELLE

PALANCA

GIUDECCA

REDENTORE

— 14 —

KEY

SYMBOLS

★ Biennale Venue

🚏 Vaporetto Stop

REFERENCE NUMBERS

These cross-refer to the exhibition listings

C/-- Collateral Event

L/-- The Laboratory of the Future (offsite)

N/-- National Pavilion

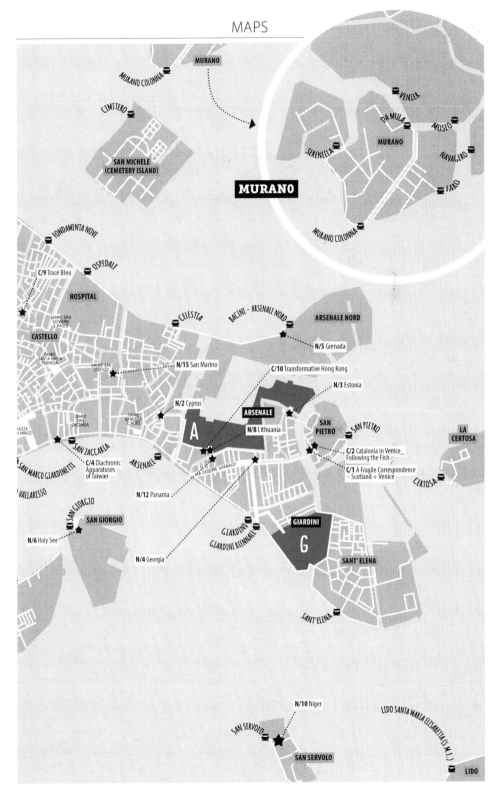

EXHIBITION LISTINGS

Venice and all its architecture awaits you…

The listings are divided into sections. Each has its own introduction and contents list. Within this, each exhibition has its own page, with all the info a visitor could need, including dates, hours, map reference, description, photo, quotes, and visiting tips. There is an alphabetical index at the end for finding things fast.

LISTINGS SECTIONS

Visitors explore 'Dangerous Liaisons', in the long Corderie section of the Arsenale
Photo by Andrea Avezzù. Courtesy La Biennale di Venezia

THE LABORATORY OF THE FUTURE

18th International Architecture Exhibition

Every Venice Biennale has its overall tone set by a thematic exhibition, known officially as the 'International Exhibition'. This year the curator is Ghanaian-Scottish architect, educator and novelist Lesley Lokko, who has chosen the name 'The Laboratory of the Future'. The show explores themes of decolonization and decarbonization, with a focus on Africa and the African Diaspora. It has two locations, the Giardini's Central Pavilion, and various spaces within the nearby Arsenale historic dockyard. There's also a related project on mainland Mestre, in the old military complex of Forte Marghera.

SECTION CONTENTS

FORCE MAJEURE

'Shade', at the entrance to 'Force Majeure', is part of the Curator's Rooms strand

Photo by Matteo de Mayda. Courtesy La Biennale di Venezia

THE LABORATORY OF THE FUTURE

CURATED BY:

Lesley Lokko

EXHIBITORS:

Features over 80 international participants, listed on p. 27–28

GIARDINI   MAP REF **[G]** P. **15**   *GIARDINI PLAN P.* **12**

Venue: Giardini della Biennale (Central Pavilion), Castello
Vaporetto: Giardini; Giardini Biennale

ARSENALE   MAP REF **[A]** P. **15**   *ARSENALE PLAN P.* **13**

Venue: Arsenale (Corderie), Castello
Vaporetto: Arsenale

MESTRE   MAP REF **[L/1]** P. **14**   *MESTRE PLAN P.* **29**

Venue: Forte Marghera, Via Forte Marghera 30, Mestre, Venice 30173
Public transport: Mestre is across the causeway on the mainland. Regular buses and tram T1 go from Piazzale Roma. Trains from Venice's Santa Lucia station (vaporetto stop Ferrovia) also stop there

---

➲ FROM THE INTRODUCTION BY LESLEY LOKKO, CURATOR:

'For the first time ever, the spotlight has fallen on Africa and the African Diaspora, that fluid and enmeshed culture of people of African descent that now straddles the globe. What do we wish to say? How will what we say change anything? And, perhaps most importantly of all, how will what we say interact with and infuse what 'others' say, so that the exhibition is not a single story, but multiple stories that reflect the vexing, gorgeous kaleidoscope of ideas, contexts, aspirations, and meanings that is every voice responding to the issues of its time?

'It is often said that culture is the sum total of the stories we tell ourselves, about ourselves. Whilst it is true, what is missing in the statement is any acknowledgement of who the 'we' in question is. In architecture particularly, the dominant voice has historically been a singular, exclusive voice, whose reach and power ignores huge swathes of humanity – financially, creatively, conceptually – as though we have been listening and speaking in one tongue only. The 'story' of architecture is therefore incomplete. Not wrong, but incomplete. It is in this context particularly that exhibitions matter. They are a unique moment in which to augment, change, or re-tell a story, whose audience and impact is felt far beyond the physical walls and spaces that hold it. What we say publicly matters because it is the ground on which change is built, in tiny increments as well as giant leaps.'

labiennale.org/en/architecture/2023

➕ CURATED BY: Lesley Lokko ORGANIZED BY: La Biennale di Venezia CHAIRED BY: Roberto Cicutto

VISITING

DATES: 20 May–26 Nov 2023

GIARDINI HOURS: 20 May–30 Sep: Tue–Sun 11:00–19:00. 1 Oct–26 Nov: Tue–Sun 10:00–18:00. Last entry 15 mins before closing

ARSENALE HOURS: As Giardini, except 20 May–30 Sep there is late opening on Fri and Sat until 20:00

FORTE MARGHERA HOURS: Tue–Sun 12:00–20:00

CLOSED: Mon (except 22 May, 14 Aug, 4 Sep, 16 Oct, 30 Oct, 20 Nov)

ADMISSION: Biennale ticket. Available online only. See p. 9 for full details. Forte Marghera is free

TICKET INFO: labiennale. org/en/architecture/2023/ information#tickets

> ❝ **In architecture particularly, the dominant voice has historically been a singular, exclusive voice, whose reach and power ignores huge swathes of humanity – financially, creatively, conceptually – as though we have been listening and speaking in one tongue only** ❞
>
> *Lesley Lokko, curator of 'The Laboratory of the Future'*

DANGEROUS LIAISONS
Serge Attukwei Clottey's immense yellow plastic tapestry 'Time and Chance' –
made from discarded cooking oil containers – shrouds the waters of the Gaggiandre
Photo by Marco Zorzanello. Courtesy La Biennale di Venezia

THE LABORATORY OF THE FUTURE
THE CURATORIAL STRANDS

The main exhibition is divided up into several sections. Here's what's in them:

FORCE MAJEURE

Arranged throughout the Giardini's Central Pavilion, 'Force Majeure' is the show's introductory statement (though you can visit Arsenale first if you wish). It brings together 16 teams to represent a truly major force – or 'force majeure' – in African and Diasporic architecture. From Adjaye Associates to Kéré Architecture, they highlight the evolving nature of contemporary practice and its potential to shape the world.

DANGEROUS LIAISONS

The exhibition continues in the Arsenale complex with a section titled 'Dangerous Liaisons'. The 37 exhibitors here range through individuals, medium-sized firms, and smaller teams. They cover a wide range of approaches such as film, investigative journalism, adaptive reuse, and grassroots community-based practice.

CURATOR'S ROOMS

These are four areas of 'Force Majeure', in the Central Pavilion. Three – 'Shade', 'Portico', and 'Loom' – are large installations. The fourth, 'Archive of the Future', presents a dense array of archival material. Two further spaces in the Arsenale – 'Portico' and 'Square' – are not described as curator's rooms, but provide similar atmospheric pausing points.

GUESTS FROM THE FUTURE

Dotted throughout both the Giardini and the Arsenale are installations by 22 young African and Diasporan practitioners, dubbed 'Guests from the Future'. These emerging talents provide a glimpse into the concerns and ambitions of a new generation, reflecting the evolving nature of architectural discourse and the increasing influence of previously marginalized cultures.

DANGEROUS LIAISONS
An installation by Office 24-7 and Lemon Pebble Architects forms part of the 'Dangerous Liaisons' section
Photo by Andrea Avezzù. Courtesy La Biennale di Venezia

CURATOR'S ROOMS
'Loom', a red-walled room lined with texts and a lattice-like ceiling installation, in the Central Pavilion
Photo by Matteo de Mayda. Courtesy La Biennale di Venezia

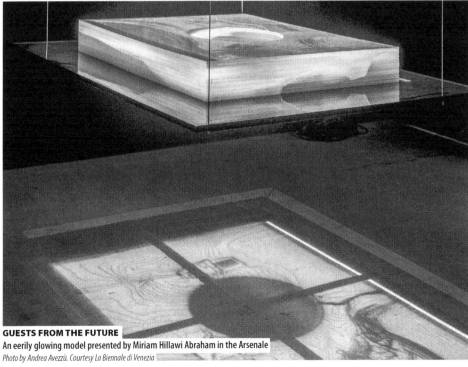

GUESTS FROM THE FUTURE
An eerily glowing model presented by Miriam Hillawi Abraham in the Arsenale
Photo by Andrea Avezzù. Courtesy La Biennale di Venezia

THE LABORATORY OF THE FUTURE
THE CURATORIAL STRANDS
Continued from previous page

CURATOR'S SPECIAL PROJECTS

These participants collaborated with Lesley Lokko and her team to create work on three themes: the relationship between memory and architecture; the impact of climate change on land practices and food production; and the intersection of gender, architecture, and performance. All are at the Arsenale, and – in a first for the Architecture Biennale – all the curatorial projects are given equal prominence to the 'main' exhibition. 'Guests from the Future' is also a wider part of this strand.

SPECIAL PARTICIPATIONS

Also at the Arsenale are three 'special' participants, invited to add a tangential artistic perspective. The trio are Amos Gitaï, an acclaimed filmmaker; Rhael 'LionHeart' Cape, architecture's first poet laureate; and large-scale architectural photographer James Morris.

OUTDOOR INSTALLATIONS

Three exhibitors also have breakout installations in the open air. Around the Arsenale's Gaggiandre (covered docks), Adjaye Associates and Sumayya Vally & Moad Musbahi present more thoughts from 'Force Majeure'. Adjaye's blackened timber pyramid beside the historic crane is particularly striking. It's called 'Kwaee', which means 'forest' in Ghana's Twi dialect. From 'Dangerous Liaisons' emerges Serge Attukwei Clottey, with the immense yellow plastic tapestry 'Time and Chance'. It's made of the 'Kufuor' containers found throughout Ghana – which arrive from Europe as cooking oil canisters and are reused to store water and petrol. Furthest flung is a meeting house by Emmanuel Pratt for Sweet Water Foundation, at Forte Marghera on mainland Mestre. Intended as a modular social space, it can seat up to 250 people and is open to the public.

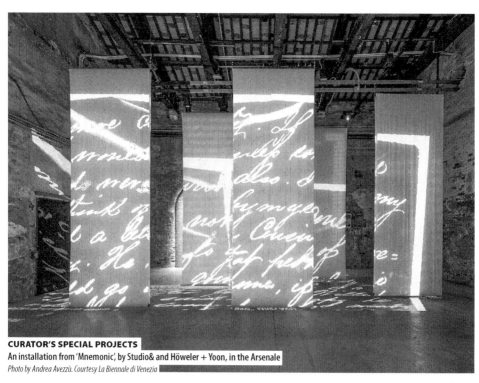

CURATOR'S SPECIAL PROJECTS
An installation from 'Mnemonic', by Studio& and Höweler + Yoon, in the Arsenale
Photo by Andrea Avezzù. Courtesy La Biennale di Venezia

SPECIAL PARTICIPATIONS
One of photographer James Morris's large-scale images in the Arsenale
Photo by Andrea Avezzù. Courtesy La Biennale di Venezia

OUTDOOR INSTALLATIONS
The 'Kwaee' pavilion by Adjaye Associates, next to the Arsenale's historic crane
Photo by Andrea Avezzù. Courtesy La Biennale di Venezia

THE LABORATORY OF THE FUTURE
GIARDINI EXHIBITORS PLAN

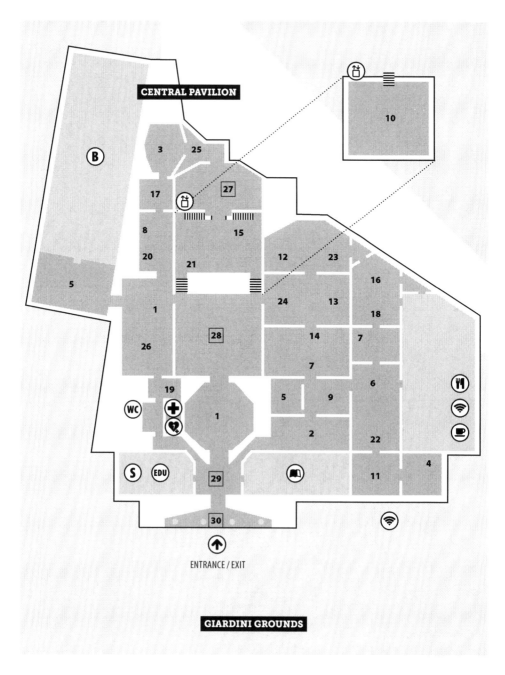

KEY

 AED Defibrillator

 Biennale Educational

 Biennale Library

 Biennale Sessions

 Bookshop

 Entrance / Exit

First Aid

Lift / Escalator

 Restaurant

 Snacks

Stairs

Toilets

 Wifi Point

MAIN EXHIBITION

FORCE MAJEURE

Central Pavilion

1 Adjaye Associates
   (also in Gaggiandre, Arsenale)

2 atelier masōmī

3 BASIS with GKZ

4 Cave_bureau

5 Hood Design Studio

6 Ibrahim Mahama

7 Kéré Architecture

8 Koffi & Diabaté Architectes

9 MASS Design Group

10 Olalekan Jeyifous

11 SOFTLAB@PSU

12 Studio Sean Canty

13 Sumayya Vally & Moad Musbahi
   (also in Gaggiandre, Arsenale)

14 Thandi Loewenson

15 Theaster Gates Studio

16 urban american city (urbanAC)

Gaggiandre, Arsenale
(see next page)

A Adjaye Associates

B Sumayya Vally & Moad Musbahi

CURATOR'S SPECIAL PROJECTS

Guests from the Future

17 Ainslee Alem Robson

18 Banga Colectivo

19 Blac Space

20 Cartografia Negra

21 Courage Dzidula Kpodo
   with Postbox Ghana

22 Faber Futures

23 Folasade Okunribido

24 New South

25 Riff Studio

26 Tanoa Sasraku

CURATOR'S ROOMS

27 Archive of the Future

28 Loom

29 Portico

30 Shade

❝ **For the first time ever, the spotlight has fallen on Africa and the African Diaspora, that fluid and enmeshed culture of people of African descent that now straddles the globe** ❞

Lesley Lokko, curator of 'The Laboratory of the Future'

THE LABORATORY OF THE FUTURE
ARSENALE EXHIBITORS PLAN

MAIN EXHIBITION

DANGEROUS LIAISONS

Corderie & Artiglierie

1 AD—WO
2 AMAA Collaborative Architecture Office for Research and Development
3 Andrés Jaque/Office for Political Innovation
4 Paulo Tavares / autonoma
5 BDR Bureau and carton123 architecten
6 DAAR — Alessandro Petti and Sandi Hilal
7 David Wengrow and Eyal Weizman with Forensic Architecture and The Nebelivka Project
8 Dream The Combine
9 Dualchas Architects
10 Estudio A0
11 Flores & Prats Architects
12 Gbolade Design Studio
13 Gloria Cabral and Sammy Baloji with Cécile Fromont
14 GRANDEZA STUDIO
15 Huda Tayob
16 kate otten architects
17 Killing Architects
18 Le laboratoire d'architecture

19 Liam Young
20 Low Design Office
21 MMA Design Studio
22 Neri&Hu Design and Research Office
23 Office 24-7 and Lemon Pebble Architects
24 orizzontale
25 Rahul Mehrotra with Ranjit Hoskote
26 SCAPE Landscape Architecture
27 Stephanie Hankey, Michael Uwemedimo and Jordan Weber
28 Studio Barnes
29 Serge Attukwei Clottey (also in Gaggiandre)
30 Suzanne Dhaliwal
31 Sweet Water Foundation (also in Forte Marghera)
32 The Funambulist
33 Twenty Nine Studio / Sammy Baloji
34 Ursula Biemann
35 White Arkitekter
36 Wolff Architects
37 ZAO / standardarchitecture

CURATOR'S SPECIAL PROJECTS

Food, Agriculture & Climate Change

38 BothAnd Group
39 Gloria Pavita
40 Margarida Waco

Gender & Geography

41 Caroline Wanjiku Kihato, Clare Loveday and Mareli Stolp in collaboration with Sedinam Awo Tsegah
42 Gugulethu Sibonelelo Mthembu
43 Ines Weizman
44 J. Yolande Daniels

Mnemonic

45 Adjaye Associates with Kiran Nadar Museum of Art
46 Craig McClenaghan Architecture
47 Looty
48 Studio& and Höweler + Yoon. Mabel O. Wilson, J. Meejin Yoon and Eric Höweler in collaboration with Josh Begley and Gene Han

Special Participations

49 Amos Gitaï
50 James Morris
51 Rhael 'LionHeart' Cape

Guests from the Future

52 Anusha Alamgir
53 Arinjoy Sen
54 Aziza Chaouni Projects
55 Black Females in Architecture
56 Dele Adeyemo
57 Elementerre with Nzinga Biegueng Mboup and Chérif Tall
58 Ibiye Camp
59 Juergen Strohmayer and Glenn DeRoché
60 Lauren-Loïs Duah
61 Miriam Hillawi Abraham
62 Moe+Art Architecture
63 Rashid Ali Architects Curator's Rooms

64 Portico
65 Square

CORDERIE

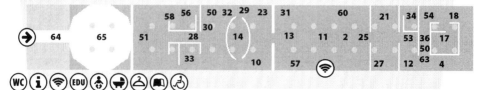

OUTDOOR INSTALLATIONS

GAGGIANDRE

Force Majeure

A   Adjaye Associates
B   Sumayya Vally &
     Moad Musbahi

Dangerous Liaisons

C   Serge Attukwei Clottey

FORTE MARGHERA

Dangerous Liaisons

D   Sweet Water Foundation

KEY

(♥)	AED Defibrillator
(EDU)	Biennale Educational
(S)	Biennale Sessions
(📖)	Bookshop
(⌣)	Cloakroom
(🚼)	Courtesy Stroller
(♿)	Courtesy Wheelchair
(→)	Entrance / Exit
(👪)	Family Area
(✚)	First Aid
(i)	Information Point
(🍴)	Restaurant
(CARS)	Shuttle Cars
(☕)	Snacks
(WC)	Toilets
(📶)	Wifi Point

FORTE MARGHERA (mainland)

MESTRE (🚌)

ACTV TRAM / BUS STOP
Forte Marghera

Walking route

VENICE

Sweet Water Foundation
D

FORTE MARGHERA

GAGGIANDRE (covered dockyards area of Arsenale)

B
B
A   C
GAGGIANDRE
B
(CARS)
CRANE (☕)
Uzbek Pavilion
Italian Pavilion
(WC)

(CARS)

NATIONAL PAVILIONS

39   40
38   39
(☕)(🍴)(✚)(♥)
44
(WC) **ARTIGLIERIE**   43   (📶)
42   41
45
(EDU)   48   46
(S)   47

CORDERIE CONTINUED

	55	24	52 61	15	8	50	62				
65	20 9		19 50 6	26 1	35	49 65	
	37	7	(📶) 16	22	3 50	5 59	

THE LABORATORY OF THE FUTURE
A-Z OF EXHIBITOR BIOGS

Where they are currently based, followed by their place and dates of birth

AD—WO
New York, USA
Emanuel Admassu (b. Addis Ababa, Ethiopia, 1983); Jen Wood (b. Melbourne, Australia, 1984)

Adjaye Associates
Accra, Ghana; London, UK; New York, USA
Sir David Adjaye OBE (b. Dar es Salaam, Tanzania, 1966)

Ainslee Alem Robson
Los Angeles, USA
Ainslee Alem Robson (b. Cleveland, USA, 1993)

AMAA Collaborative Architecture Office for Research and Development
Venice, Italy
Marcello Galiotto (b. Arzignano, Italy, 1986); Alessandra Rampazzo (b. Mirano, Italy, 1986)

Amos Gitaï
Paris, France; Haifa, Israel and internationally
Amos Gitaï (b. Haifa, Israel, 1950)

Andrés Jaque / Office for Political Innovation
New York, USA; Madrid, Spain
Andrés Jaque (b. Madrid, Spain, 1971)

Anusha Alamgir
London, UK; Dhaka, Bangladesh; New York, USA
Anusha Alamgir (b. Dhaka, Bangladesh, 1995)

Arinjoy Sen
London, UK
Arinjoy Sen (b. Kolkata, India, 1996)

atelier masōmī
Niamey, Niger
Mariam Issoufou Kamara (b. St Etienne, France, 1979)

Aziza Chaouni Projects
Fez, Morocco; Toronto, Canada
Aziza Chaouni (b. Fez, Morocco, 1977)

Banga Colectivo
Luanda, Angola; Lisbon, Portugal
Yolana Lemos (b. Luanda, Angola, 1995); Kátia Mendes (b. Lubango, Angola, 1995); Elsimar Freitas (b. Luanda, Angola, 1993); Mamona Duca (b. Luanda, Angola, 1993); Gilson Mendes (b. Malanje, Angola, 1993)

BASIS with GKZ
New York, USA; Los Angeles, USA; London, UK
Zenna Tavares (b. London, UK, 1986); Kibwe Tavares (b. London, UK, 1983); Gaika Tavares (b. London, UK, 1982); Eli Bingham (b. New York, USA, 1993); Emily Mackevicius (b. Massachusetts, USA, 1989)

BDR Bureau and carton123 architecten
Turin, Italy; Brussels, Belgium
Simona Della Rocca (b. Moncalieri, Italy, 1985); Alberto Bottero (b. Cuneo, Italy, 1984); Els Van Meerbeek (b. Leuven, Belgium, 1974); Joost Raes (b. Leuven, Belgium, 1979)

Blac Space
Johannesburg, Republic of South Africa
Kgaugelo Lekalakala (b. Mpumalanga, Republic of South Africa, 1994)

Black Females in Architecture
London, UK
Akua Danso (b. London, UK, 1991); Selasi Setufe (b. London, UK, 1990); Neba Sere (b. Cologne, Germany, 1990); Ama Ofori-Darko (b. London, UK, 1998)

BothAnd Group
Dublin, Ireland
Jarek Adamczuk (b. Zamość, Poland, 1992); Alice Clarke (b. Summerhill, Ireland, 1992); Andrew Ó Murchú (b. Limerick, Ireland, 1991); Kate Rushe (b. Galway, Ireland, 1992)

Caroline Wanjiku Kihato, Clare Loveday and Mareli Stolp in collaboration with Sedinam Awo Tsegah
Nairobi, Kenya; Johannesburg, Pretoria, Republic of South Africa
Caroline Wanjiku Kihato (b. Nairobi, Kenya, 1971); Clare Loveday (b. Johannesburg, Republic of South Africa, 1967); Mareli Stolp (b. Pretoria, Republic of South Africa, 1980). In collaboration with Sedinam Awo Tsegah

Cartografia Negra
São Paulo, Brazil
Raissa de Oliveira (b. São Bernardo do Campo, Brazil, 1993); Carolina Vieira (b. São Paulo, Brazil, 1993); Pedro Alves (b. São Paulo, Brazil, 1992)

Cave_bureau
Nairobi, Kenya
Kabage Karanja (b. Nairobi, Kenya, 1979); Stella Mutegi (b. Nairobi, Kenya, 1979)

Courage Dzidula Kpodo with Postbox Ghana
Accra, Ghana; Boston, USA; Milan, Italy
Courage Kpodo (b. Kumasi, Ghana, 1999); Manuela Nebuloni (b. Rho, Italy, 1986); Nana Ofosu Adjei (b. Accra, Ghana, 1993)

Craig McClenaghan Architecture
Johannesburg, Republic of South Africa
Craig McClenaghan (b. East-London, South Africa, 1977)

DAAR — Alessandro Petti and Sandi Hilal
Stockholm, Sweden; Bethlehem, Israel

David Wengrow and Eyal Weizman with Forensic Architecture and The Nebelivka Project
London, UK
Eyal Weizman (b. Haifa, Israel, 1970); David Wengrow (b. UK, 1972)

Dele Adeyemo
London, UK; Lagos, Nigeria
Olubamidele Adeyemo (b. Kaduna, Nigeria, 1985)

Dream The Combine
Ithaca, Minneapolis, USA
Jennifer Newsom (b. Norwich, USA, 1979); Tom Carruthers (b. Vancouver, Canada, 1978)

Dualchas Architects
Isle of Skye, Glasgow, UK
Neil Stephen (b. Glasgow, UK, 1969); Alasdair Stephen (b. Glasgow, UK, 1969); Rory Flyn (b. Inverness, UK, 1978)

Elementerre with Nzinga Biegueng Mboup and Chérif Tall
Dakar, Gandigal, Senegal
Doudou Deme (b. Dakar, Senegal, 1982); Nzinga Biegueng Mboup (b. Maputo, Mozambique, 1989); Chérif Tall (b. Dakar, Senegal, 1991)

Estudio A0
Quito, Ecuador
Ana María Durán Calisto (b. Quito, Ecuador, 1971); Jaskran Kalirai (b. Derby, UK, 1974)

Faber Futures
London, UK
Natsai Audrey Chieza (b. Harare, Zimbabwe, 1985)

Flores & Prats Architects
Barcelona, Spain
Eva Prats (b. Barcelona, Spain, 1965); Ricardo Flores (b. Buenos Aires, Argentina, 1965)

Folasade Okunribido
London, UK
Folasade Okunribido (b. Lincoln, England, 1995)

Gbolade Design Studio
London, UK
Tara Gbolade (b. Kaduna, Nigeria, 1985); Lanre Gbolade (b. Ota, Nigeria, 1985)

Gloria Cabral and Sammy Baloji with Cécile Fromont
Guarda do Embau, Brazil; Brussels, Belgium; New Haven, USA
Gloria Cabral (b. São Paulo, Brazil, 1982); Sammy Baloji (b. Lubumbashi, Democratic Republic of the Congo, 1978); Cécile Fromont (b. Schœlcher, Martinique, 1980)

Gloria Pavita
Cape Town, Republic of South Africa
Gloria Pavita (b. Kinshasa, Democratic Republic of Congo, 1995)

GRANDEZA STUDIO
Madrid, Spain; Sydney, Australia
Amaia Sánchez-Velasco (b. Salamanca, Spain, 1985); Jorge Valiente Oriol (b. Madrid, Spain, 1984); Gonzalo Valiente Oriol (b. Madrid, Spain, 1982)

Gugulethu Sibonelelo Mthembu
Johannesburg, Republic of South Africa
Gugulethu Sibonelelo Mthembu (b. Soweto, South Africa, 1992)

Hood Design Studio
Oakland, USA
Walter Hood (b. Fort Bragg, USA, 1958); Alma Du Solier (b. Monterrey, Mexico, 1972)

Huda Tayob
Cape Town, Republic of South Africa; Manchester, UK
Huda Tayob (b. Cape Town, Republic of South Africa, 1986)

Ibiye Camp
London, UK
Ibiye Camp (b. London, UK, 1991)

Ibrahim Mahama
Tamale, Ghana
Ibrahim Mahama (b. Tamale, Ghana, 1987)

Ines Weizman
London, UK
Ines Weizman (b. Leipzig, Germany, 1973)

J. Yolande Daniels
New York, Boston, Los Angeles, USA
J. Yolande Daniels (b. New York, USA, 1962)

James Morris
Bwlchllan, Wales, UK
James Morris (b. Griffithstown, Wales, UK, 1963)

Juergen Strohmayer and Glenn DeRoché
Accra, Ghana
Juergen Strohmayer (b. Istanbul, Turkey, 1990); Glenn DeRoché (b. New York, USA, 1985)

kate otten architects
Johannesburg, Republic of South Africa
Kate Otten (b. Durban, Republic of South Africa, 1964)

Kéré Architecture
Berlin, Germany
Diébédo Francis Kéré (b. Gando, Burkina Faso, 1965)

Killing Architects
Rotterdam, Netherlands
Alison Killing (b. Newcastle upon Tyne, UK, 1979)

Koffi & Diabaté Architectes
Abidjan, Ivory Coast
Guillaume Koffi (b. Gagnoa, Ivory Coast; 1959); Issa Diabaté (b. Abidjan, Ivory Coast, 1969)

Lauren-Loïs Duah
London, UK
Lauren-Loïs Duah (b. Mulhouse, France, 1998)

Le laboratoire d'architecture
Geneva, Switzerland
Vanessa Lacaille (b. Paris, France, 1980); Mounir Ayoub (b. Tunis, Tunisia, 1980)

Liam Young
Los Angeles, USA
Liam Young (b. Australia, 1979)

Looty
London, UK
Chidirim Nwaubani (b. London, UK, 1988)

Low Design Office
Austin, USA; Tema, Ghana
Ryan Bollom (b. Spring, USA, 1979); DK Osseo-Asare (b. State College, USA 1980)

Margarida Waco
Stockholm, Sweden; London, UK
Margarida Waco (b. Cabinda; Angola, 1992)

MASS Design Group
Boston, USA; Kigali, Rwanda
Christian Benimana (b. Rwanda, 1982)

Miriam Hillawi Abraham
Addis Ababa, Ethiopia
Miriam Hillawi Abraham (b. Addis Ababa, Ethiopia, 1994)

MMA Design Studio
Johannesburg, Republic of South Africa
Mphethi Morojele (b. Maseru, Lesotho, 1963)

Moe+Art Architecture
Lagos, Nigeria
Papa Omotayo (b. Ijebu Ode, Nigeria, 1975); Mosun Ogunbanjo (b. Lagos, Nigeria, 1959); Dami Akinniyi (b. Lagos, Nigeria, 1987)

Neri&Hu Design and Research Office
Shanghai, People's Republic of China
Lyndon Neri / Guo Xi-En (b. Ozamiz, Philippines, 1965); Rossana Hu / Hu Ru-Shan (b. Kaohsiung, China, 1968)

New South
Paris, France
Meriem Chabani (b. Algiers, Algeria, 1989); John Edom (b. Portsmouth, UK, 1983)

Office 24-7 and Lemon Pebble Architects
Johannesburg, Republic of South Africa
Nabeel Essa (b. Polokwane, Republic of South Africa, 1971); Tanzeem Razak (b. Benoni, Republic of South Africa, 1973)

Olalekan Jeyifous
Brooklyn, USA
Olalekan Jeyifous (b. Ibadan, Nigeria, 1977)

orizzontale
Rome, Italy
Nasrin Mohiti Asli (b. Rome, Italy, 1987); Margherita Manfra (b. Rome, Italy, 1985); Giuseppe Grant (b. Caserta, Italy, 1987); Roberto Pantaleoni (b. Rome, Italy, 1987); Stefano Ragazzo (b. Rome, Italy, 1987); Juan López Cano (b. Cardeña, Spain, 1981); Jacopo Ammendola (b. Fiesole, Italy, 1983)

Paulo Tavares / autonoma
Brasília, Brazil
Paulo Tavares (b. Campinas, Brazil, 1980)

Rahul Mehrotra with Ranjit Hoskote
Mumbai, India; Boston, USA
Rahul Mehrotra (b. New Delhi, India, 1959); Ranjit Hoskote (b. Mumbai, India, 1969)

Rashid Ali Architects Curator's Rooms
Hargeisa, Somaliland; London, UK
Rashid Ali (b. Hargeisa, Somaliland, 1978)

Rhael 'LionHeart' Cape
London, UK
Rhael 'LionHeart' Cape, Hon FRIBA (b. London, UK, 1987)

Riff Studio
New York, USA
Rekha Auguste-Nelson (b. Philadelphia, USA, 1991); Farnoosh Rafaie (b. Los Angeles, USA, 1988); Isabel Strauss (b. Chicago, USA, 1990)

SCAPE Landscape Architecture
New York, USA
Kate Orff (b. Silver Springs, USA, 1971)

Serge Attukwei Clottey
Accra, Ghana
Serge Attukwei Clottey (b. Accra, Ghana, 1985)

SOFTLAB@PSU
State College, USA
Felecia Davis (b. Michigan, USA, 1959)

Stephanie Hankey, Michael Uwemedimo and Jordan Weber
Berlin, Germany and internationally; Port Harcourt, Nigeria and internationally; New York City, Boston, St. Louis, Minneapolis, USA
Stephanie Hankey (b. Manchester, UK, 1973); Michael Uwemedimo (b. Calabar, Nigeria, 1972); Jordan Weber (b. Des Moines, USA, 1985)

Studio Barnes
Miami, USA
Germane Barnes (b. Chicago, USA, 1985)

Studio Sean Canty
Boston, USA
Sean Canty (b. Philadelphia, USA, 1987)

Studio& and Höweler + Yoon. Mabel O. Wilson, J. Meejin Yoon and Eric Höweler in collaboration with Josh Begley and Gene Han
New York, Boston, USA
Mabel O. Wilson (b. Neptune, USA, 1963); J. Meejin Yoon (b. Seoul, Korea, 1972); Eric Höweler (b. Cali, Colombia, 1972). In collaboration with Josh Begley and Gene Han

Sumayya Vally & Moad Musbahi
Johannesburg, Republic of South Africa; London, UK; Tripoli, Libya; New York, USA
Sumayya Vally (b. Pretoria, Republic of South Africa, 1990); Moad Musbahi

Suzanne Dhaliwal
Croatia; UK
Suzanne Dhaliwal (b. Birmingham, UK, 1982)

Sweet Water Foundation
Chicago, USA
Emmanuel Pratt (b. Richmond, USA, 1977)

Tanoa Sasraku
London, UK
Tanoa Sasraku (b. Plymouth, UK, 1995)

Thandi Loewenson
London, UK
Thandi Loewenson (b. Harare, Zimbabwe, 1989)

The Funambulist
Paris, France
Léopold Lambert (b. Paris, France, 1985)

Theaster Gates Studio
Chicago, USA
Theaster Gates (b. Chicago, USA, 1973)

Twenty Nine Studio / Sammy Baloji
Brussels, Belgium
Sammy Baloji (b. Lubumbashi, Democratic Republic of Congo, 1978)

urban american city (urbanAC)
New York, USA
Toni L. Griffin (b. Chicago, USA, 1964)

Ursula Biemann
Zurich, Switzerland and internationally
Ursula Biemann (b. Zurich, Switzerland, 1955)

White Arkitekter
Sweden
Alexandra Hagen (b. Malmö, Sweden, 1972)

Wolff Architects
Cape Town, Republic of South Africa
Ilze Wolff (b. Cape Town, Republic of South Africa, 1980); Heinrich Wolff (b. Johannesburg, Republic of South Africa, 1970)

ZAO / standardarchitecture
Beijing, People's Republic of China
Zhang Ke (b. Anhui, People's Republic of China, 1970)

THE LABORATORY OF THE FUTURE
A-Z OF EXHIBITOR LOCATIONS

The area and page numbers refer to the exhibition plans on the previous pages

EXHIBITOR	AREA	REF	CURATORIAL STRAND	PLAN PAGE
AD—WO	Arsenale	1	Dangerous Liaisons	p. 28
Adjaye Associates	Giardini	1	Force Majeure	p. 26
	Arsenale	A	Outdoor installation	p. 29
Adjaye Associates with Kiran Nadar Museum of Art	Arsenale	45	Mnemonic	p. 28
Ainslee Alem Robson	Giardini	17	Guests from the Future	p. 26
AMAA Collaborative Architecture Office for Research and Development	Arsenale	2	Dangerous Liaisons	p. 28
Amos Gitaï	Arsenale	49	Special Participations	p. 28
Andrés Jaque / Office for Political Innovation	Arsenale	3	Dangerous Liaisons	p. 28
Anusha Alamgir	Arsenale	52	Guests from the Future	p. 28
Arinjoy Sen	Arsenale	53	Guests from the Future	p. 28
atelier masōmi	Giardini	2	Force Majeure	p. 26
Aziza Chaouni Projects	Arsenale	54	Guests from the Future	p. 28
Banga Colectivo	Giardini	18	Guests from the Future	p. 26
BASIS with GKZ	Giardini	3	Force Majeure	p. 26
BDR Bureau and carton123 architecten	Arsenale	5	Dangerous Liaisons	p. 28
Blac Space	Giardini	19	Guests from the Future	p. 26
Black Females in Architecture	Arsenale	55	Guests from the Future	p. 28
BothAnd Group	Arsenale	38	Food, Agriculture & Climate Change	p. 28
Caroline Wanjiku Kihato, Clare Loveday and Mareli Stolp in collaboration with Sedinam Awo Tsegah	Arsenale	41	Gender & Geography	p. 28
Cartografia Negra	Giardini	20	Guests from the Future	p. 26
Cave_bureau	Giardini	4	Force Majeure	p. 26
Courage Dzidula Kpodo with Postbox Ghana	Giardini	21	Guests from the Future	p. 26
Craig McClenaghan Architecture	Arsenale	46	Mnemonic	p. 28
DAAR — Alessandro Petti and Sandi Hilal	Arsenale	6	Dangerous Liaisons	p. 28
David Wengrow and Eyal Weizman with Forensic Architecture and The Nebelivka Project	Arsenale	7	Dangerous Liaisons	p. 28
Dele Adeyemo	Arsenale	56	Guests from the Future	p. 28
Dream The Combine	Arsenale	8	Dangerous Liaisons	p. 28
Dualchas Architects	Arsenale	9	Dangerous Liaisons	p. 28
Elementerre with Nzinga Biegueng Mboup and Chérif Tall	Arsenale	57	Guests from the Future	p. 28
Estudio A0	Arsenale	10	Dangerous Liaisons	p. 28
Faber Futures	Giardini	22	Guests from the Future	p. 26
Flores & Prats Architects	Arsenale	11	Dangerous Liaisons	p. 28
Folasade Okunribido	Giardini	23	Guests from the Future	p. 26
Gbolade Design Studio	Arsenale	12	Dangerous Liaisons	p. 28
Gloria Cabral and Sammy Baloji with Cécile Fromont	Arsenale	13	Dangerous Liaisons	p. 28
Gloria Pavita	Arsenale	39	Food, Agriculture & Climate Change	p. 28
GRANDEZA STUDIO	Arsenale	14	Dangerous Liaisons	p. 28
Gugulethu Sibonelelo Mthembu	Arsenale	42	Gender & Geography	p. 28
Hood Design Studio	Giardini	5	Force Majeure	p. 26
Huda Tayob	Arsenale	15	Dangerous Liaisons	p. 28
Ibiye Camp	Arsenale	58	Guests from the Future	p. 28
Ibrahim Mahama	Giardini	6	Force Majeure	p. 26

INTERNATIONAL EXHIBITION

EXHIBITOR	AREA	REF	CURATORIAL STRAND	PLAN PAGE
Ines Weizman	Arsenale	43	Gender & Geography	p. 28
J. Yolande Daniels	Arsenale	44	Gender & Geography	p. 28
James Morris	Arsenale	50	Special Participations	p. 28
Juergen Strohmayer and Glenn DeRoché	Arsenale	59	Guests from the Future	p. 28
kate otten architects	Arsenale	16	Dangerous Liaisons	p. 28
Kéré Architecture	Giardini	7	Force Majeure	p. 26
Killing Architects	Arsenale	17	Dangerous Liaisons	p. 28
Koffi & Diabaté Architectes	Giardini	8	Force Majeure	p. 26
Lauren-Loïs Duah	Arsenale	60	Guests from the Future	p. 28
Le laboratoire d'architecture	Arsenale	18	Dangerous Liaisons	p. 28
Liam Young	Arsenale	19	Dangerous Liaisons	p. 28
Looty	Arsenale	47	Mnemonic	p. 28
Low Design Office	Arsenale	20	Dangerous Liaisons	p. 28
Margarida Waco	Arsenale	40	Food, Agriculture & Climate Change	p. 28
MASS Design Group	Giardini	9	Force Majeure	p. 26
Miriam Hillawi Abraham	Arsenale	61	Guests from the Future	p. 28
MMA Design Studio	Arsenale	21	Dangerous Liaisons	p. 28
Moe+Art Architecture	Arsenale	62	Guests from the Future	p. 28
Neri&Hu Design and Research Office	Arsenale	22	Dangerous Liaisons	p. 28
New South	Giardini	24	Guests from the Future	p. 26
Office 24-7 and Lemon Pebble Architects	Arsenale	23	Dangerous Liaisons	p. 28
Olalekan Jeyifous	Giardini	10	Force Majeure	p. 26
orizzontale	Arsenale	24	Dangerous Liaisons	p. 28
Paulo Tavares / autonoma	Arsenale	4	Dangerous Liaisons	p. 28
Rahul Mehrotra with Ranjit Hoskote	Arsenale	25	Dangerous Liaisons	p. 28
Rashid Ali Architects Curator's Rooms	Arsenale	63	Guests from the Future	p. 28
Rhael 'LionHeart' Cape	Arsenale	51	Special Participations	p. 28
Riff Studio	Giardini	25	Guests from the Future	p. 26
SCAPE Landscape Architecture	Arsenale	26	Dangerous Liaisons	p. 28
Serge Attukwei Clottey	Arsenale	29	Dangerous Liaisons	p. 28
	Arsenale	C	Outdoor installation	p. 29
SOFTLAB@PSU	Giardini	11	Force Majeure	p. 26
Square	Arsenale	65	Force Majeure	p. 28
Stephanie Hankey, Michael Uwemedimo and Jordan Weber	Arsenale	27	Force Majeure	p. 28
Studio Barnes	Arsenale	28	Force Majeure	p. 28
Studio Sean Canty	Giardini	12	Force Majeure	p. 26
Studio& and Höweler + Yoon. Mabel O. Wilson, J. Meejin Yoon & Eric Höweler in collaboration w/ Josh Begley & Gene Han	Arsenale	48	Mnemonic	p. 28
Sumayya Vally & Moad Musbahi	Giardini	13	Force Majeure	p. 26
	Arsenale	B	Outdoor installation	p. 29
Suzanne Dhaliwal	Arsenale	30	Dangerous Liaisons	p. 28
Sweet Water Foundation	Arsenale	31	Dangerous Liaisons	p. 28
	Mestre	D	Outdoor installation	p. 29
Tanoa Sasraku	Giardini	26	Guests from the Future	p. 26
Thandi Loewenson	Giardini	14	Force Majeure	p. 26
The Funambulist	Arsenale	32	Dangerous Liaisons	p. 28
Theaster Gates Studio	Giardini	15	Force Majeure	p. 26
Twenty Nine Studio / Sammy Baloji	Arsenale	33	Dangerous Liaisons	p. 28
urban american city (urbanAC)	Giardini	16	Force Majeure	p. 26
Ursula Biemann	Arsenale	34	Dangerous Liaisons	p. 28
White Arkitekter	Arsenale	35	Dangerous Liaisons	p. 28
Wolff Architects	Arsenale	36	Dangerous Liaisons	p. 28
ZAO / standardarchitecture	Arsenale	37	Dangerous Liaisons	p. 28

A pillar from Israel's 'Queendom' show being transported to the German pavilion, which repurposes architectural leftovers from the 2022 Art Biennale

Photo © ARCH+ Summacumfemmer Büro Juliane Greb. Courtesy Pavilion of Germany

NATIONAL PAVILIONS

Exhibitions by countries invited to participate in the official Biennale

Originally, each country had its own Giardini building or 'pavilion', so their presentations became known as 'National Pavilions'. Then more countries took part, their shows spread to the Arsenale and temporary venues across city, and the official Biennale term became 'National Participations'. Colloquially, everyone still calls them National Pavilions; it's even on the signage. This year there are 63 of them, listed on the page numbers below.

SECTION CONTENTS

ALBANIA

EXHIBITION TITLE:

Untimely Meditations or: How we learn to live in synthesized realities

CURATED BY:

Heramarte (Era Merkuri, Martin Gjoleka)

EXHIBITORS:

Heramarte (Martin Gjoleka, Era Merkuri) with Ani Marku and Geraldo Prendushi

ARSENALE MAP REF **[A]** P. **15**   *ARSENALE PLAN P. 13*

Venue: Arsenale, Castello
Vaporetto: Arsenale

⊙ Explores how computer rendering technology is shaping our views of public spaces. The curators, along with architect Ani Marku and 3D digital artist Geraldo Prendushi, present their observations of two derelict spaces in Tirana – an empty stadium and an artificial lake – and expand the discussion to encompass the Anthropocene era. Collaborating with experts from various fields, the project includes workshops, discussions, and dining lectures to further examine the connection between humans, the environment, and technology in urban landscapes.

⊕ COMMISSIONER: Elva Margariti, Minister of Culture of the Republic of Albania

VISITING

DATES: 20 May–26 Nov 2023

HOURS: 20 May–30 Sep: Tue, Wed, Thu, Sun 11:00–19:00; Fri, Sat, 11:00–20:00. 1 Oct–26 Nov: Tue–Sun 10:00–18:00. Last entry 15 mins before closing

CLOSED: Mon (except 22 May, 14 Aug, 4 Sep, 16 Oct, 30 Oct, 20 Nov)

ADMISSION: Biennale ticket. Available online only. See p. 9 for full details

TICKET INFO: labiennale. org/en/architecture/2023/ information#tickets

> **❝ By observing and mapping urban spaces, we question the boundary between the natural and artificial ❞**
> *Curatorial statement*

An aptly abandoned-looking setting for this digital exploration of disused spaces
Photo by Andrea Avezzù. Courtesy La Biennale di Venezia

ARGENTINA

EXHIBITION TITLE:

El Futuro del Agua

CURATED BY:

Diego Arraigada

ARSENALE MAP REF **[A]** P. **15**   *ARSENALE PLAN P. 13*

Venue: Arsenale, Castello
Vaporetto: Arsenale

➲ The pavilion is pervaded by the impression of blue fluid, although it is actually a single immersive hue filling the space up to thigh height. Above, randomly positioned light tables evoke the feeling of a current. These form part of a curatorial 'water glossary', with images relevant to each term presented on the tables. Visitors wander through this fluid space, engaging with the past and present of water in Argentina and the architectural projects related to it; the aim is to promote reflection on future actions. Exiting the pavilion, visitors find themselves in the real water of the canals and lagoon in Venice, highlighting the power and fragility of water.

➕ COMMISSIONER: Paula Vázquez

VISITING

DATES: 20 May–26 Nov 2023

HOURS: 20 May–30 Sep: Tue, Wed, Thu, Sun 11:00–19:00; Fri, Sat, 11:00–20:00. 1 Oct–26 Nov: Tue–Sun 10:00–18:00. Last entry 15 mins before closing

CLOSED: Mon (except 22 May, 14 Aug, 4 Sep, 16 Oct, 30 Oct, 20 Nov)

ADMISSION: Biennale ticket. Available online only. See p. 9 for full details

TICKET INFO: labiennale. org/en/architecture/2023/ information#tickets

❝ **Argentina has a rich and privileged relationship with water, with very important worldwide resources of drinking water** ❞

Paula Vázquez, Commissioner

The lower part of the exhibition space is bathed in blue light
Photo by Marco Zorzanello. Courtesy La Biennale di Venezia

AUSTRALIA

EXHIBITION TITLE:

Unsettling Queenstown

CURATED BY:

Ali Gumillya Baker, Anthony Coupe, Emily Paech, Julian Worrall, Sarah Rhodes

GIARDINI MAP REF **[G]** P. **15**   *GIARDINI PLAN P. 12*

Venue: Giardini della Biennale, Castello
Vaporetto: Giardini; Giardini Biennale

⊙ A multi-sensory installation exploring the relationship between people and the environment, particularly in the context of colonialism and resource extraction. It focuses on Queenstown, a place where the environmental and social costs of extractive practices are evident. By examining the town's past traumas and present energies, the creative directors draw connections between similar 'Queenstowns' worldwide, highlighting their significance as symbols of decolonial struggles. The exhibition aims to reveal hidden stories of pre-colonial lands and contribute to a future-oriented dialogue in Venice.

architecture.com.au/venice-biennale

⊕ COMMISSIONER: Janet Holmes à Court AC

VISITING

DATES: 20 May–26 Nov 2023
HOURS: 20 May–30 Sep: Tue–Sun 11:00–19:00. 1 Oct–26 Nov: Tue–Sun 10:00–18:00. Last entry 15 mins before closing
CLOSED: Mon (except 22 May, 14 Aug, 4 Sep, 16 Oct, 30 Oct, 20 Nov)
ADMISSION: Biennale ticket. Available online only. See p. 9 for full details
TICKET INFO: labiennale.org/en/architecture/2023/information#tickets

> 66 **There are Queenstowns all over the former British Empire … It is a place both local and global** 99
>
> *Curatorial statement*

Model of the arched belvedere of the Empire Hotel in Queenstown on lutruwita/Tasmania
Photo by Matteo de Mayda. Courtesy La Biennale di Venezia

AUSTRIA

EXHIBITION TITLE:

Partecipazione / Beteiligung

CURATORS / EXHIBITORS:

AKT (Fabian Antosch, Gerhard Flora, Max Hebel, Adrian Judt, Julia Klaus, Lena Kohlmayr, Philipp Krummel, Gudrun Landl, Lukas Lederer, Susanne Mariacher, Christian Mörtl, Philipp Oberthaler, Charlie Rauchs, Helene Schauer, Kathrin Schelling, Philipp Stern and Harald Trapp) and Hermann Czech

GIARDINI MAP REF **[G]** P. **15**   *GIARDINI PLAN P. 12*

Venue: Giardini della Biennale, Castello
Vaporetto: Giardini; Giardini Biennale

➲ In a critique of the Biennale's spread into Venice's urban fabric, the curators proposed building a temporary scaffold bridge over the Giardini wall to nearby Sant'Elena, allowing locals free access to an 'assembly room' in half of the symmetrical Austrian pavilion. However, this idea – and an alternative idea to re-open a bricked-up door in the Giardini wall – were rejected by the Biennale authorities. As a result, only half of the bridge was built, and half the pavilion has been left empty.

labiennale2023.at/en

➕ COMMISSIONER: The Arts and Culture Division of the Federal Ministry for Art, Culture, the Civil Service and Sport of Austria

VISITING

DATES: 20 May–26 Nov 2023

HOURS: 20 May–30 Sep: Tue–Sun 11:00–19:00. 1 Oct–26 Nov: Tue–Sun 10:00–18:00. Last entry 15 mins before closing

CLOSED: Mon (except 22 May, 14 Aug, 4 Sep, 16 Oct, 30 Oct, 20 Nov)

ADMISSION: Biennale ticket. Available online only. See p. 9 for full details

TICKET INFO: labiennale. org/en/architecture/2023/ information#tickets

> 66 **Now the vacancy of the assembly room and the Biennale's spatial policy will become the central exhibits** 99

Hermann Czech, curator. From AKT & Hermann Czech newsletter, May 2023

View over the wall to Sant'Elena, from the incomplete scaffolding bridge
Photo © Clelia Cadamuro. Courtesy Pavilion of Austria

BAHRAIN *(Kingdom of)*

EXHIBITION TITLE:
Sweating Assets

CURATED BY:
Maryam Aljomairi, Latifa Alkhayat

EXHIBITORS:
Alanood Alkhayat, Alya Ali, Chenyue xdd Dai, Dr. Reem Al Maella, Dr. Waleed Alzubari, Hajar Budhahi, Hsin-Ying Huang, Hussain Almosawi, Khushi Nansi, Latifa Alkhayat, Marwa Al Koheji, Maryam Al Noami, Maryam Aljomairi, Melad Alfulaij, Nada Almulla, Nasser Al Zayani, Natalie Pearl, Nujud Alhussain, Rabeeya Abduljabbar, Saleh Jamsheer, Sara Ali, Sasha McKinlay, Shan-Chun Wen, Vijay Rajkumar, Yi-Liang Ko, Zicheng Xu

GIARDINI MAP REF **[G]** P. **15**   *GIARDINI PLAN P.* **12**

Venue: Giardini della Biennale, Castello
Vaporetto: Giardini; Giardini Biennale

○ Buildings act as vessels of condensation, collecting moisture from the atmosphere, but this water is often wasted. The exhibition proposes using these untapped reservoirs to alleviate water scarcity and reduce reliance on desalination. By working with existing systems, the show advocates for adaptive resource management in Bahrain's challenging climate.

sweatingassets.bh

○ COMMISSIONER: Shaikh Khalifa bin Ahmad Al Khalifa, Bahrain Authority for Culture and Antiquities

VISITING
DATES: 20 May–26 Nov 2023
HOURS: 20 May–30 Sep: Tue–Sun 11:00–19:00. 1 Oct–26 Nov: Tue–Sun 10:00–18:00. Last entry 15 mins before closing
CLOSED: Mon (except 22 May, 14 Aug, 4 Sep, 16 Oct, 30 Oct, 20 Nov)
ADMISSION: Biennale ticket. Available online only. See p. 9 for full details
TICKET INFO: labiennale. org/en/architecture/2023/ information#tickets

❝ With a projected 5°C temperature rise by the turn of the century, the region is at the extremities of both water shortage and heat ❞
Curatorial statement

A new look at old water resources
Photo by Andrea Avezzù. Courtesy La Biennale di Venezia

BELGIUM

EXHIBITION TITLE:

In Vivo

CURATED BY:

Bento and Vinciane Despret

EXHIBITORS:

Bento et Vinciane Despret with the collaboration of Corentin Mahieu, Juliette Salme, Corentin Mullender, PermaFungi, BC materials, Sonian Wood Coop

GIARDINI MAP REF **[G]** P. **15**   *GIARDINI PLAN P.* ***12***

Venue: Giardini della Biennale, Castello
Vaporetto: Giardini; Giardini Biennale

➲ In Vivo challenges our current production system by exploring architectural alternatives using organic materials from living organisms. The installation experiments with uncultivated soil and mycelium on a large scale, demonstrating their potential in the construction field. The central room features a wooden structure made with locally sourced mycelium, wood, and soil, allowing visitors to experience their sensory and poetic qualities. It acts as a laboratory for the future of sustainable building, emphasizing regional materials and promoting new pathways for living materials in Belgium and beyond.

belgianpavilion.be

➕ COMMISSIONER: Fédération Wallonie-Bruxelles

VISITING

DATES: 20 May–26 Nov 2023

HOURS: 20 May–30 Sep: Tue–Sun 11:00–19:00. 1 Oct–26 Nov: Tue–Sun 10:00–18:00. Last entry 15 mins before closing

CLOSED: Mon (except 22 May, 14 Aug, 4 Sep, 16 Oct, 30 Oct, 20 Nov)

ADMISSION: Biennale ticket. Available online only. See p. 9 for full details

TICKET INFO: labiennale. org/en/architecture/2023/information#tickets

❝ We are proposing an alliance with mushrooms, which can constitute a highly available, sustainable, renewable material ❞

Curatorial statement

A huge structure made with locally sourced mycelium, wood, and soil
Photo by Matteo de Mayda. Courtesy La Biennale di Venezia

BRAZIL

EXHIBITION TITLE:

Terra (Earth)

CURATED BY:

Gabriela de Matos and Paulo Tavares

EXHIBITORS:

Ana Flávia Magalhães Pinto, Ayrson Heráclito, Day Rodrigues, with participation by Vilma Patricia, Fissura, Ilê Axé Iyá Nassô Oká (Casa Branca do Engenho Velho), Juliana Vicente, Mbya-Guarani Indigenous People, Tukano, Arawak and Maku Indigenous Peoples, Tecelãs do Alaká (Ilê Axé Opô Afonjá), Thierry Oussou, Vídeo nas Aldeias

GIARDINI   MAP REF **[G]** P. **15**   *GIARDINI PLAN P. 12*

Venue: Giardini della Biennale, Castello
Vaporetto: Giardini; Giardini Biennale

⟫ The floor of the pavilion is covered with earth, to evoke the traditions of indigenous territories, Quilombola homes, and candomblé ceremonies. At the entrance, Brazilian public housing elements with the sankofa symbol contrast with the modernist features of the 1964 pavilion. The exhibition is divided into two galleries, and challenges the notion that Brasilia was built in an isolated, uninhabited area.

⊕ COMMISSIONER: José Olympio da Veiga Pereira, president of the Fundação Bienal de São Paulo

VISITING

DATES: 20 May–26 Nov 2023

HOURS: 20 May–30 Sep: Tue–Sun 11:00–19:00. 1 Oct–26 Nov: Tue–Sun 10:00–18:00. Last entry 15 mins before closing

CLOSED: Mon (except 22 May, 14 Aug, 4 Sep, 16 Oct, 30 Oct, 20 Nov)

ADMISSION: Biennale ticket. Available online only. See p. 9 for full details

TICKET INFO: labiennale. org/en/architecture/2023/ information#tickets

❝ **The concept of earth is of great importance in the cosmologies, philosophies, and narratives of the Indigenous and Afro-Brazilian populations** ❞

Gabriela de Matos, exhibitor

The pavilion features a floor covered smoothly with earth
Photo by Matteo de Mayda. Courtesy La Biennale di Venezia

BULGARIA

EXHIBITION TITLE:

Education is the movement from darkness to light

CURATED BY:

Boris Tikvarski

EXHIBITORS:

Boris Tikvarski, Alexander Dumarey, Bojidara Valkova, Mariya Gyaurova, Mike Fritsch and Kostadin Kokalanov

CITY MAP REF **[N/1]** P. **14–15**

Venue: Centro Culturale don Orione Artigianelli (Sala del Tiziano), Zattere, Dorsoduro 919

Vaporetto: Zattere

➡ Focusing on depopulation and aging populations, this project aims to encourage discussion rather than solve the issues. It includes photographs of abandoned school buildings by Belgian photographer Alexandre Dumarey, highlighting the scale of Bulgaria's demographic problem. According to the team's statistics, Bulgaria has the largest population decline globally, with a projected 22% further decline over the next 30 years. The exhibition aims to address similar issues affecting other countries in the former Eastern Bloc.

➕ COMMISSIONER: Alexander Staynov

VISITING

DATES: 20 May–26 Nov 2023

HOURS: 20 May–30 Sep: Wed–Mon 11:00–19:00. 1 Oct–26 Nov: Wed–Mon 10:00–18:00

CLOSED: Tue (except 23 May, 21 Nov)

ADMISSION: Free

❝ **We want to make ordinary people think more about the issue as it is up to us to try to slow down these processes affecting the whole country** ❞

Bozhidara Valkova, exhibitor

'Malomir, 2021', one of a series photographs of abandoned school buildings by Alexandre Dumarey
Image © Alexander Dumarey. Courtesy Pavilion of Bulgaria

CANADA

EXHIBITION TITLE:
Not for Sale!!

CURATED BY:
Architects Against Housing Alienation (AAHA): Adrian Blackwell, David Fortin, Matthew Soules, Sara Stevens, Patrick Stewart, Tijana Vujosevic

EXHIBITORS:
A Better Tent City Waterloo Region; Affordable Housing Association of Nova Scotia; Alex Wilson, University of Saskatchewan; At Home in the North; Atelier Big City; Bâtir son quartier; Black Urbanism TO; Canadian Cohousing Network; Centre d'ecologie urbaine de Montréal (CEUM); CP Planning; David T Fortin Architect Inc; FBM architecture – interior design – planning; Gentrification Tax Action; Grounded Architecture Inc; Haeccity Studio Architecture; Idle No More; Ipek Türeli, McGill University; Katlia Lafferty, National Indigenous Housing Network; Keele Eglinton Residents; L'OEUF Architects; Lancelot Coar, University of Manitoba; LGA Architectural Partners; Luugigyoo, Patrick R. Stewart Architect, Nisga'a Nation; Navigator Street Outreach Program; One House Many Nations; Ouri Scott, Urban Arts Architecture Inc; Parkdale Neighbourhood Land Trust; Sarah Silva, Hiyam Housing; SOCA (Studio of Contemporary Architecture); SOLO Architecture; SvN Architects and Planners; Sylvia McAdam, Windsor University; Table de concertation du Faubourg Saint-Laurent; Toronto Tiny Shelters; tuf lab; Xalek/Sekyu Siyam Chief Ian Campbell, Skwxwu7mesh Uxwumixw (Squamish Nation)

GIARDINI   MAP REF **[G]**   P. **15**   *GIARDINI PLAN P.* **12**

Venue: Giardini della Biennale, Castello
Vaporetto: Giardini; Giardini Biennale

⊙ The exhibition focuses on Canada's housing crisis, which includes issues such as unaffordability, under-housing, precarious housing, and homelessness. This crisis is influenced by speculative real estate practices and the historical displacement of Indigenous lands. The exhibition, led by Architects Against Housing Alienation (AAHA), aims to reject the current concept of property and its financially-oriented architectural implications. AAHA will collaborate with activist organizations, housing advocates, and architects to develop demands and architectural projects that address housing alienation. Their goal is to mobilize Canadians and create safer, healthier, and more equitable housing. AAHA is a curatorial collective formed especially for the Venice Biennale of Architecture and includes members from various architectural institutions. UBC SALA will be the lead organization, partnering with the University of Waterloo School of Architecture.

aaha.ca/en; canadacouncil.ca/initiatives/venice-biennale

⊕ COMMISSIONER: Canada Council for the Arts

VISITING
DATES: 20 May–26 Nov 2023
HOURS: 20 May–30 Sep: Tue–Sun 11:00–19:00. 1 Oct–26 Nov: Tue–Sun 10:00–18:00. Last entry 15 mins before closing
CLOSED: Mon (except 22 May, 14 Aug, 4 Sep, 16 Oct, 30 Oct, 20 Nov)
ADMISSION: Biennale ticket. Available online only. See p. 9 for full details
TICKET INFO: labiennale.org/en/architecture/2023/information#tickets

❝ **We believe that the roots of the housing crisis lie in the capitalist and colonialist dispossession of people from their land and homes** ❞

Curatorial statement

A sticker from the 'Not for Sale' campaign
Image courtesy Pavilion of Canada

CHILE

EXHIBITION TITLE:

Moving Ecologies

CURATED BY:

Gonzalo Carrasco, Beals Lyon Arquitectos

EXHIBITORS:

Featured projects: Baquedano Wetland Park, Batuco Marsh Nature Sanctuary Master Plan, Bicentennial High School in Maipu, Cerro Calán Observatory Park, Huasco South Coastal Border Park, INIA Intihuasi Seed Bank, Vicuña, Kaukari Urban Park, Koyaüwe Landscaping, Las Salinas Plant Laboratory, Los Batros Wetland Park, Metropolitan Park Cerros de Renca, Native Sidewalk, Quinta Normal Park, Santa Olga Park, Sustainable Gardens Providencia, Triple Impact Nursery in Patagonia. Soundscapes: Felipe Cisternas

ARSENALE MAP REF **[A]** P. **15**   *ARSENALE PLAN P. **13***

Venue: Arsenale, Castello

Vaporetto: Arsenale

⊙ 250 seed-filled spheres, representing hope and care, showcase the INIA Intihuasi Seed Bank in Vicuña, Chile, which safeguards the future of humanity through the collection and care of endemic and native species. Soundscapes recorded in nearby Puerto Varas capture the process of seed propagation.

movingecologies.com

⊕ COMMISSIONER: Cristobal Molina Baeza, Ministry of Cultures, Arts and Heritage of Chile

VISITING

DATES: 20 May–26 Nov 2023

HOURS: 20 May–30 Sep: Tue, Wed, Thu, Sun 11:00–19:00; Fri, Sat, 11:00–20:00. 1 Oct–26 Nov: Tue–Sun 10:00–18:00. Last entry 15 mins before closing

CLOSED: Mon (except 22 May, 14 Aug, 4 Sep, 16 Oct, 30 Oct, 20 Nov)

ADMISSION: Biennale ticket. Available online only. See p. 9 for full details

TICKET INFO: labiennale. org/en/architecture/2023/ information#tickets

❝ **The future will be both designed and sown, built and cultivated, made of architecture and seeds, cities and ecologies** ❞

Curatorial statement

Serried ranks of seed-filled spheres on stalks fill the exhibition space
Photo by Marco Zorzanello. Courtesy La Biennale di Venezia

CHINA *(People's Republic of)*

EXHIBITION TITLE:

Renewal: a symbiotic narrative

CURATED BY:

Ruan Xing

EXHIBITORS:

Bo Hongtao, Cai Chunyan / Liu Tao, Du Chunlan, Fan Beilei / Kong Rui / Xue Zhe, Guo Yuchen / Yang Siqi / Zhan Beidi / Jiang Boyuan / Wang Jingwen / Yang Shuo, He Jianxiang / Jiang Ying, He Mengjia, Huang Huaqing, Huang Yinwu, Jin Qiuye, Kong Yuhang / Yang Wei, Li Danfeng / Zhou Jianjia, Li Xinggang, Liu Doreen Heng, Liu Kenan / Zhang Xu, Liu Moyan / Su Peng / Ju Anqi / Ying Shijiao / Li Yuanyuan / Song Jiawei, Liu Yuyang, Long Ying, Luo Jing / Yu Borou, Meng Fanhao, Qian Shiyun, Ruan Xing / Zhang Yang, Shui Yanfei, Song Yehao, Sun Haode / Student Team SJTU, Tong Ming / Ren Guang /Guo Hongqu, Wang Dan / Li Zhibo, Wang Qiu'an, Wang Xin / Sun Yu, Wang Yan, Wang Zhuo'er, Wu Hongde / Du Qian / Rao Fujie / Wang Hao, Xu Xunjun / Zhang Xudong / Pang Lei, Yang Yongliang, Zhang Bin, Zhang Jiajing, Zhang Li / Zhao Peng / Ye Yang, Zhang Ming / Zhang Zi / Qin Shu / Su Ting, Zhang Tong / Aldo Aymonino, Zheng Xiaodi, Zhou Wei, Zhuang Shen / Ren Hao / Tang Yu / Zhu Jie, Zhuang Ziyu, Shanghai Design Week, Atelier Deshaus, Arcplus Group-ECADI (East China Architectural Design and Research Institute Co./Ltd.), Arcplus Group – Institute of Shanghai Architectural Design & Research (Co./Ltd.), CBC Building Centre, Chongqing Architectural Design Institute of Chongqing Design Group

ARSENALE MAP REF **[A]** P. **15**   *ARSENALE PLAN P. 13*

Venue: Arsenale, Castello
Vaporetto: Arsenale

❯ The exhibition consists of three chapters: 'DENSITY wonder Portraits of Plurality', 'LIVEABILITY renewal Stories of Shanghai', and 'SYMBIOSIS future Rejuvenation'. Within these, a multitude of Chinese architects and artists address how to revitalize cities while preserving cultural heritage, with an emphasis on sustainable development in both urban and rural areas. The exhibition offers insights into China's 40-year urbanization through case studies in Shanghai, where the population swiftly grew from 11 million to 25 million, and per capita living space expanded from 4.5 to 37.4 square meters. The aim is to showcase the interconnectedness of cities, people, and nature, highlighting the importance of harmonious coexistence.

➕ COMMISSIONER: China Arts and Entertainment Group Ltd (CAEG)

VISITING

DATES: 20 May–26 Nov 2023

HOURS: 20 May–30 Sep: Tue, Wed, Thu, Sun 11:00–19:00; Fri, Sat, 11:00–20:00. 1 Oct–26 Nov: Tue–Sun 10:00–18:00. Last entry 15 mins before closing

CLOSED: Mon (except 22 May, 14 Aug, 4 Sep, 16 Oct, 30 Oct, 20 Nov)

ADMISSION: Biennale ticket. Available online only. See p. 9 for full details

TICKET INFO: labiennale. org/en/architecture/2023/ information#tickets

❝ **The theme of the exhibition tells of Chinese experiments in shaping liveability in high-density environments** ❞

Curatorial statement

Pillar installation in the China pavilion's garden
Photo by Marco Zorzanello.
Courtesy La Biennale di Venezia

CROATIA

EXHIBITION TITLE:

Same as it ever was

CURATED BY:

Mia Roth, Tonči Čerina

EXHIBITORS:

Mia Roth, Tonči Čerina, Luka Fatović, Vedran Kasap, Ozana Ursić, Niko Mihaljević, Ivica Mitrović

ARSENALE   MAP REF **[A]** P. **15**   *ARSENALE PLAN P. 13*

Venue: Arsenale, Castello
Vaporetto: Arsenale

❯ The pavilion's main statement is a large sculptural installation of woven ash wood, symbolizing the interconnectedness between humans and nature. The structure originates from a collection of observatories in the Lonja wetlands – one of Europe's largest – known as the 'bestiarium'. These blend elements of nature and culture, capturing the essence of a seemingly static landscape with dramatic seasonal transformations. By studying autonomous communities in peripheral regions, the show explores living with nature and building resilience.

sameasiteverwas.hr

➕ COMMISSIONER: Ministry of Culture and Media of the Republic of Croatia

VISITING

DATES: 20 May–26 Nov 2023

HOURS: 20 May–30 Sep: Tue, Wed, Thu, Sun 11:00–19:00; Fri, Sat, 11:00–20:00. 1 Oct–26 Nov: Tue–Sun 10:00–18:00. Last entry 15 mins before closing

CLOSED: Mon (except 22 May, 14 Aug, 4 Sep, 16 Oct, 30 Oct, 20 Nov)

ADMISSION: Biennale ticket. Available online only. See p. 9 for full details

TICKET INFO: labiennale. org/en/architecture/2023/ information#tickets

❝ **The wetlands point to the capacity of nature's self-healing without our intervention or survival** ❞
Curatorial statement

A sculptural 'bestiarium', made from woven ash wood
Photo by Andrea Avezzù. Courtesy La Biennale di Venezia

CYPRUS *(Republic of)*

EXHIBITION TITLE:
From Khirokitia to Mars

CURATORS / EXHIBITORS:
Petros Lapithis, Lia Lapithi, Nikos Kouroussis,
Ioanna Ioannou Xiari, Cyprus Space Exploration Organization

CITY MAP REF **[N/2]** P. **14–15**

Venue: Associazione Culturale Spiazzi, Fondamenta
del Pistor (off Ponte Storto), Castello 3865
Vaporetto: Arsenale

❯ Examines the ancient settlements of the Cyprus Aceramic
Neolithic era, specifically Khirokitia, and takes inspiration from
this innovative civilization to envision a newly constructed
environment on Mars. The journey of early Neolithic settlers
to Cyprus reflects their ability to navigate the unknown,
demonstrating their remarkable skills and adaptability. It
raises thought-provoking questions about whether Neolithic
principles can inform future architectural thinking, and whether
the knowledge and technology of future settlers could enable
the establishment of a thriving community on another planet.

www.cyprusinvenice.org

✛ COMMISSIONER: Petros Dymiotis, Cultural Officer at the Cultural
Services of the Deputy Ministry of Culture

VISITING

DATES: 20 May–26 Nov 2023
HOURS: Tue–Sun 11:00–19:00
CLOSED: Mon
ADMISSION: Free

❝ **Space flight has
radically expanded
our knowledge of
the world around
us. But just as
ancient explorers
were drawn to the
sea, we are drawn
to the universe** ❞

*Petros Lapithis, curator. Quoted
in 'Parametric Architecture'*

Journeying from the past to the future
Image courtesy Pavilion of Republic of Cyprus ▪

CZECH *(Republic)*

EXHIBITION TITLE:

The Office for a Non-Precarious Future

CURATED BY:

Karolína Plášková

EXHIBITORS:

Eliška Pomyjová, David Neuhäusl, Jan Netušil

GIARDINI MAP REF **[G]** P. **15** *GIARDINI PLAN P.* ***12***

Venue: Giardini della Biennale, Castello
Vaporetto: Giardini; Giardini Biennale

ARSENALE MAP REF **[A]** P. **15** *ARSENALE PLAN P.* ***13***

Venue: Arsenale, Castello
Vaporetto: Arsenale

Explores the challenges faced by young architects in their jobs and asks how they can improve the world when they work in a flawed system. It is based on research revealing that nearly half of young architects work as freelancers without benefits like health insurance or social security. The show has two parts, Factory and Laboratory, representing the current difficult working conditions, and a space to imagine new solutions.

czechpavilionbiennale23.com; labiennale.ngprague.cz

COMMISSIONER: Helena Huber-Doudová

VISITING

DATES: 20 May–26 Nov 2023

GIARDINI HOURS: 20 May–30 Sep: Tue–Sun 11:00–19:00. 1 Oct–26 Nov: Tue–Sun 10:00–18:00. Last entry 15 mins before closing

ARSENALE HOURS: As Giardini, except 20 May–30 Sep there is late opening on Fri and Sat until 20:00

CLOSED: Mon (except 22 May, 14 Aug, 4 Sep, 16 Oct, 30 Oct, 20 Nov)

ADMISSION: Biennale ticket. Available online only. See p. 9 for full details

TICKET INFO: labiennale.org/en/architecture/2023/information#tickets

VISITING TIP: Due to refurbishment, the Czech and Slovak Pavilion in the Giardini is closed. It will act as a digital hub, while the actual show is housed in the Arsenale.

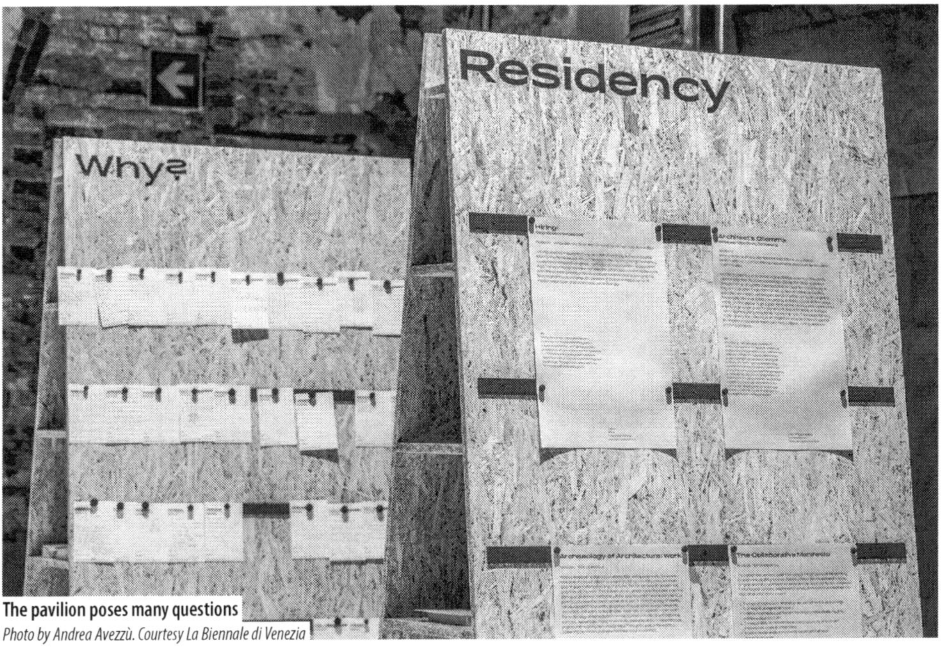

The pavilion poses many questions
Photo by Andrea Avezzù. Courtesy La Biennale di Venezia

DENMARK

EXHIBITION TITLE:
Coastal Imaginaries

CURATED BY:
Josephine Michau

EXHIBITORS:
Schønherr Landscape Architects, David Garcia, Giacomo Brusa Cattaneo, Laurits Sporon Bøving Genz, Dejle Zaradesht Mohamad, Iisa Eikaas, Katrina Wiberg, Anna Aslaug Lund and Christian Friedländer

GIARDINI   MAP REF **[G]** P. **15**   *GIARDINI PLAN P. 12*

Venue: Giardini della Biennale, Castello
Vaporetto: Giardini; Giardini Biennale

⬦ Considers innovative solutions for rising sea levels, drawing inspiration from nature. A highlight is the 'Copenhagen Islands' proposal, by landscape architecture firm Schønherr, to update the city's current urban plan by utilizing islets that naturally occur in the delta between seawater and rainwater. The show also includes a dramatic depiction of a future coastal landscape created by set designer Christian Friedländer, allowing visitors to experience climate change first hand.

dac.dk/en/exhibitions/coastal-imaginaries

⊕ COMMISSIONER: Kent Martinussen, Danish Architecture Centre

VISITING

DATES: 20 May–26 Nov 2023

HOURS: 20 May–30 Sep: Tue–Sun 11:00–19:00. 1 Oct–26 Nov: Tue–Sun 10:00–18:00. Last entry 15 mins before closing

CLOSED: Mon (except 22 May, 14 Aug, 4 Sep, 16 Oct, 30 Oct, 20 Nov)

ADMISSION: Biennale ticket. Available online only. See p. 9 for full details

TICKET INFO: labiennale. org/en/architecture/2023/ information#tickets

❝ **Humans are contributing to many of the crises we are facing today … the architects who design our physical surroundings play a vital role in this** ❞

Josephine Michau, curator

A future coastal landscape created by set designer Christian Friedländer
Photo by Matteo de Mayda. Courtesy La Biennale di Venezia

EGYPT

EXHIBITION TITLE:

NiLab – The Nile as Laboratory

CURATORS:

Ahmed Sami Abd Elrahman, Marina Tornatora, Ottavio Amaro, Ghada Farouk, Moataz Samir

EXHIBITORS:
**Ain-Shams University of Cairo, Faculty of Engineering (Egypt);
Università Mediterranea Reggio Calabria, dArTe Department (Italy)**

GIARDINI MAP REF **[G]** P. **15** *GIARDINI PLAN P. 12*

Venue: Giardini della Biennale, Castello
Vaporetto: Giardini; Giardini Biennale

> ❂ Through projections and immersive displays, the exhibition traces the Nile's path from Lake Nasser to the Mediterranean, highlighting its unique intertwining of nature, civilization, and history. At the centre stands a representation of an ancient Egyptian 'Sun Boat', symbolic of rebirth. Displays of projects, from urban life to archaeological landscapes, emphasize the significance of the Nile in Egypt's history and its role as a source of life. Finally, a captivating film by Ahmed Yasser, 'Grand Tour on Nile', highlights the significance of the river.

⊕ COMMISSIONER: Egyptian Ministry of Culture; Egyptian Academy; National Organization for Urban Harmony

VISITING

DATES: 20 May–26 Nov 2023

HOURS: 20 May–30 Sep: Tue–Sun 11:00–19:00. 1 Oct–26 Nov: Tue–Sun 10:00–18:00. Last entry 15 mins before closing

CLOSED: Mon (except 22 May, 14 Aug, 4 Sep, 16 Oct, 30 Oct, 20 Nov)

ADMISSION: Biennale ticket. Available online only. See p. 9 for full details

TICKET INFO: labiennale. org/en/architecture/2023/ information#tickets

> 66 **The river must remain the centre of life and development in Egypt, through research and cooperation between countries** 99
> *Curatorial statement*

A representation of an ancient Egyptian 'Sun Boat'
Photo by Matteo de Mayda. Courtesy La Biennale di Venezia

ESTONIA

EXHIBITION TITLE:

Home Stage

CURATORS / EXHIBITORS:

Aet Ader, Mari Möldre, Arvi Anderson

CITY MAP REF **[N/3]** P. **14–15**

Venue: Castello 96 (at the base of the ramp to the Giardino delle Vergini), Salizada Streta, Castello 96
Vaporetto: Giardini; San Pietro di Castello

→ Tackles the contrast between home as a basic necessity and home as a commodity. The show takes place in a rented apartment near the Arsenale, serving as a stage for various housing stories. Estonian performers will live in the apartment for a month each, enacting scripted and unscripted scenes. Visitors begin their journey outside, resting on wooden daybeds before entering the apartment. The entrance wall will be continuously painted and repainted by each performer. The exhibition explores the challenges of secure housing and features surreal and poetic performances on modern living.

homestage.ee

⊕ COMMISSIONER: Raul Järg

VISITING

DATES: 18 May–29 Nov 2023
HOURS: May: Tue–Sun 11:00–14:30, 15:30–19:00.
Jun–Nov: Wed–Sun 11:00–14:30, 15:30–19:00
CLOSED: May: Mon. Jun–Nov: Mon–Tue
ADMISSION: Free

> 66 **Visitors will find themselves in front of a closed door that will be unlocked to welcome them into an empty room save for four vacuum cleaners blowing dust bunnies around** 99

Curatorial statement. Quoted in 'Azure'

'Depression : Growth', one of several paired images evoking the project's themes
Image © Arvi Anderson, Kertin Vasser. Courtesy Pavilion of Estonia

FINLAND *(Aalto Pavilion)*

EXHIBITION TITLE:

Huussi – Imagining the Future History of Sanitation

CURATED BY:

Arja Renell, The Dry Collective

EXHIBITORS:

The Dry Collective: Antero Jokinen, Emmi Keskisarja, Barbara Motta, Arja Renell, Eero Renell, Janne Teräsvirta

GIARDINI MAP REF **[G]** P. **15**   *GIARDINI PLAN P. **12***

Venue: Giardini della Biennale, Castello
Vaporetto: Giardini; Giardini Biennale

→ The Finns imagine that it's 2043, and flushing lavatories no longer exist. Instead they are replaced by public toilets producing valuable compost, as already seen in Helsinki's return to historical night-soil collections. It focuses on the Finnish composting toilet called 'huussi', commonly used in rural areas and vacation homes. Flushable toilets consume 30% of water in developed nations, so by adopting models that generate fertilizers, societies can conserve resources. An 'excavated' ceramic loo outside amusingly symbolizes this future world.

✛ COMMISSIONER: Katarina Siltavuori, Archinfo – Information Centre for Finnish Architecture

VISITING

DATES: 20 May–26 Nov 2023

HOURS: 20 May–30 Sep: Tue–Sun 11:00–19:00. 1 Oct–26 Nov: Tue–Sun 10:00–18:00. Last entry 15 mins before closing

CLOSED: Mon (except 22 May, 14 Aug, 4 Sep, 16 Oct, 30 Oct, 20 Nov)

ADMISSION: Biennale ticket. Available online only. See p. 9 for full details

TICKET INFO: labiennale.org/en/architecture/2023/information#tickets

❝ **The flushing toilet is a perfect product of the consumerist era … wasteful, globally unequal, and ecocidal** ❞

Katarina Siltavuori, Commissioner

The show houses a very public toilet (non-flushing, of course)
Photo by Matteo de Mayda. Courtesy La Biennale di Venezia

FRANCE

EXHIBITION TITLE:
Ball Theater

CURATED BY:
Muoto and Georgi Stanishev

GIARDINI　MAP REF **[G]** P. **15**　　　　*GIARDINI PLAN P. 12*

Venue: Giardini della Biennale, Castello
Vaporetto: Giardini; Giardini Biennale

➡ The French pavilion houses a theatre in the form of a giant silvery disco ball. Visitors can walk through the architectural installation, engaging with its sights and sounds, as it guides their gaze and transports them into various imaginative realms. The space will also host parties and collective experiments, celebrating rebirth after the aborted previous edition. It's a subtle nod to the history of Ball Culture that developed in Harlem in New York City in the 1920s and 1930s. The exhibition aims to create a sensory experience through sight, sound, and theatrical architecture, with the globe-shaped space serving as a venue for interaction between performers and the audience. The adjoining rooms feature recycled objects, evoking hope, nostalgia, and a future rooted in the past.

➕ COMMISSIONER: Institut Français with the Ministry of Europe and Foreign Affairs and the Ministry of Culture

VISITING

DATES: 20 May–26 Nov 2023
HOURS: 20 May–30 Sep: Tue–Sun 11:00–19:00. 1 Oct–26 Nov: Tue–Sun 10:00–18:00. Last entry 15 mins before closing
CLOSED: Mon (except 22 May, 14 Aug, 4 Sep, 16 Oct, 30 Oct, 20 Nov)
ADMISSION: Biennale ticket. Available online only. See p. 9 for full details
TICKET INFO: labiennale.org/en/architecture/2023/information#tickets

> 66 **It reflects our contrasting feelings of hope and nostalgia. Our desire to rebuild a future that belongs to the past by recycling a host of found objects** 99
>
> *Curatorial statement*

Just part of France's giant disco ball
Photo by Matteo de Mayda. Courtesy La Biennale di Venezia

GEORGIA

EXHIBITION TITLE:

January, February, March

CURATED BY:

Gigi Shukakidze, Tinatin Gurgenidze, Otar Nemsadze

EXHIBITORS:

Tbilisi Architecture Biennale, Gigi Shukakidze, Tinatin Gurgenidze, Otar Nemsadze, Giorgi Vardiashvili, Aleksandre Soselia, Stefano Tornieri, Lado Kandashvili, Giorgi Qartvelishvili, Elene Pasuri, Tato Kotetishvili

CITY MAP REF **[N/4]** P. **14–15**

Venue: Il Giardino Bianco Art Space, Via Giuseppe Garibaldi, Castello 1814
Vaporetto: Arsenale; Giardini

⊘ Explores the connection between time, energy, and the environment, using water reservoirs as symbols of political and climate change. It focuses on a flooded settlement in the Dusheti region of Georgia, caused by the construction of a hydropower plant to generate electricity for Tbilisi in the 1980s. The settlement's history, including the migration of residents and submergence of landmarks, is examined. The project poses questions about the temporary nature of our environmental impact, and the cost of disrupting established orders.

⊕ COMMISSIONER: Magda Guruli

VISITING

DATES: 20 May–26 Nov 2023
HOURS: 20 May–30 Sep: Tue–Sun 11:00–19:00. 1 Oct–26 Nov: Tue–Sun 10:00–18:00
CLOSED: Mon (except 22 May, 14 Aug, 4 Sep, 16 Oct, 30 Oct, 20 Nov)
ADMISSION: Free

❝ What are the costs of disrupting an order to create a new one? Can we take water as a determinant of order? ❞

Curatorial statement

The pavilion focuses on water reservoirs
Photo © Gigi Shukakidze. Courtesy Pavilion of Georgia

GERMANY

EXHIBITION TITLE:

Open for Maintenance – Wegen Umbau geöffnet

CURATED BY:

ARCH+ / SUMMACUMFEMMER / BÜRO JULIANE GREB
(Anne Femmer, Franziska Gödicke, Juliane Greb, Christian Hiller, Petter Krag, Melissa Makele, Anh-Linh Ngo, Florian Summa)

EXHIBITORS:

Agriluska (Luca Vallese); Assemblea Sociale per la Casa (Chiara Buratti); Bellevue di Monaco eG (Barbara Bergau, Grisi Ganzer, Till Hofmann, Denijen Pauljevic) with Hirner & Riehl architekten und stadtplaner BDA; Centro Sociale Rivolta (Elena Carraro, Filippo Lunian); ConstructLab (Patrick Hubmann, Alexander Römer, Peter Zuiderwijk); CRCLR House with Concular (Annabelle von Reutern), Die Zusammenarbeiter & TRNSFRM eG (Christian Schöningh), Impact Hub (Sascha Stremming), LXSY Architekten (Kim Le Roux, Margit Sichrovsky); Giorgio de Finis (RIF – Museo delle Periferie); Gustavo Fijalkow; Forward Dance Company / LOFFT – DAS THEATER; German Pavilion for Biennale Arte 2022: Relocating a Structure (Yilmaz Dziewior, Maria Eichhorn, Ellen Strittmatter); Haus der Materialisierung – Zentrum für klimaschonende Ressourcennutzung with Berliner Stadtmission (Sofie Göppl Leon), FahrArt Atelier (Benjamin Känel), Kostümkollektiv (Katrin Wittig), Kunst-Stoffe e.V. (Jan-Micha Garma, Rhea Gleba, Corinna Vosse), Mitkunstzentrale (Rahel Jakob, Julie Teuber, Nora Wilhelm), mrtz Forschungswerkstatt (Moritz Wermelskirch), Ort-schafft-Material (Jannis Schiefer, Elena Stranges), stefan is doing things (Stefan Klopfer), STREETWARE saved item (Alice Fassina), Studio Patric Dreier, ZUsammenKUNFT Berlin eG (Kim Gundlach, Andrea Hofmann); Institute of Radical Imagination (Marco Baravalle, Emanuele Braga, Gabriella Riccio) and Anna Rispoli, in cooperation with S.a.L.E. Docks; Kotti & Co (Tashy Endres, Sandy Kaltenborn); Laboratorio Occupato Morion; Rebiennale/ R3B (Tommaso Cacciari, Giulio Grillo); Alessandro Schiattarella; Giovanna Silva with Angelo Boriolo (Boris); Working Group Sanitärwende with Eawag (Michel Riechmann), Finizio–Future Sanitation (Florian Augustin, Tom Kühne), German Toilet Organization, KanTe – Kollektiv für angepasste Technik (Ariane Krause, Johanna Moser, Eleftheria Xenikaki) and Sina Kamala, klo:lektiv (Sabine Bongers-Römer, Katharina Ciax, Martine Kayser), Leibniz-Institut für Gemüse- und Zierpflanzenbau (Stefan Karlowsky), NetSan, P2GreeN, urin*all (Leonie Roth, Luisa Tschumi), VaLoo

---

GIARDINI MAP REF **[G]** P. **15**   *GIARDINI PLAN P.* **12**

Venue: Giardini della Biennale, Castello
Vaporetto: Giardini; Giardini Biennale

⊙ In a Biennale first, this project repurposes building supplies from over 40 pavilions and exhibitions of the previous year's Art Biennale. Each remnant has its own QR ode, and is listed in an online brochure. Highlighting the debate around maintenance and repair, it explores ideas for re-use and recycling, including a functioning composting lavatory (something of a theme this year). It critically examines the huge resources invested in such temporary events, and questions their overall value.

archplus.net/de/open-for-maintenance

⊕ COMMISSIONER: Federal Ministry for Housing, Urban Development and Building

---

VISITING

DATES: 20 May–26 Nov 2023

HOURS: 20 May–30 Sep: Tue–Sun 11:00–19:00. 1 Oct–26 Nov: Tue–Sun 10:00–18:00. Last entry 15 mins before closing

CLOSED: Mon (except 22 May, 14 Aug, 4 Sep, 16 Oct, 30 Oct, 20 Nov)

ADMISSION: Biennale ticket. Available online only. See p. 9 for full details

TICKET INFO: labiennale. org/en/architecture/2023/ information#tickets

> ❝ **A large number of national pavilions are lending support, making demolition material from their exhibitions available for reuse** ❞
>
> *Curatorial statement*

Outside the pavilion
Photo © ARCH+ Summacumfemmer Büro Juliane Greb. Courtesy Pavilion of Germany

GRAND DUCHY OF LUXEMBOURG

EXHIBITION TITLE:

Down to Earth

CURATED BY:

Francelle Cane, Marija Marić

EXHIBITORS:

Francelle Cane, Marija Marić in collaboration with Armin Linke and Lev Bratishenko with the contributions of Jane Mah Hutton, Anastasia Kubrak, Amelin Ng, Bethany Rigby, and Fred Scharmen

ARSENALE MAP REF **[A]** P. **15**   *ARSENALE PLAN P.* **13**

Venue: Arsenale, Sale d'Armi, 1st Floor, Castello

Vaporetto: Arsenale

⊙ Critically examines space mining's impact on the environment and society, questioning the privatization of space and the exploitation of celestial bodies. It explores the material aspects of space mining, including logistics, infrastructure, and workers, and their connection to geopolitical power structures. Transforming the pavilion into a lunar laboratory, the exhibition reveals hidden aspects of space mining.

venicebiennale.kulturlx.lu

⊕ COMMISSIONER: Kultur | lx — Arts Council Luxembourg and Luca — Luxembourg Center for Architecture, on behalf of Ministry of Culture

VISITING

DATES: 20 May–26 Nov 2023

HOURS: 20 May–30 Sep: Tue, Wed, Thu, Sun 11:00–19:00; Fri, Sat, 11:00–20:00. 1 Oct–26 Nov: Tue–Sun 10:00–18:00. Last entry 15 mins before closing

CLOSED: Mon (except 22 May, 14 Aug, 4 Sep, 16 Oct, 30 Oct, 20 Nov)

ADMISSION: Biennale ticket. Available online only. See p. 9 for full details

TICKET INFO: labiennale. org/en/architecture/2023/ information#tickets

❝ The unbridled imagination of extractive growth has, quite literally, transcended the boundaries of the Earth ❞

Curatorial statement

The pavilion has been transformed into a lunar mining lab

Photo by Marco Zorzanello. Courtesy La Biennale di Venezia

GREAT BRITAIN

EXHIBITION TITLE:
Dancing Before the Moon

CURATED BY:
Jayden Ali, Joseph Henry, Meneesha Kellay and Sumitra Upham

EXHIBITORS:
Yussef Agbo-Ola, Jayden Ali, Mac Collins, Shawanda Corbett, Madhav Kidao, Sandra Poulson

GIARDINI MAP REF **[G]** P. **15**   *GIARDINI PLAN P.* **12**
Venue: Giardini della Biennale, Castello
Vaporetto: Giardini; Giardini Biennale

→ A look at how everyday rituals within diasporic communities can shape architecture and the built environment. The curators aim to influence British architecture towards collectivity and community-building. Each room has an installation by a different artist referencing their culture, such as giant sculptures made of blue Angolan soap. The pavilion also includes film and music celebrating minority lives, notably a raucous soundtrack of garage and grime music that resounds across the Giardini.

venicebiennale.britishcouncil.org/dancing-moon-british-pavilion-2023

⊕ COMMISSIONER: Sevra Davis, Director of Architecture Design Fashion at the British Council

VISITING

DATES: 20 May–26 Nov 2023

HOURS: 20 May–30 Sep: Tue–Sun 11:00–19:00. 1 Oct–26 Nov: Tue–Sun 10:00–18:00. Last entry 15 mins before closing

CLOSED: Mon (except 22 May, 14 Aug, 4 Sep, 16 Oct, 30 Oct, 20 Nov)

ADMISSION: Biennale ticket. Available online only. See p. 9 for full details

TICKET INFO: labiennale. org/en/architecture/2023/ information#tickets

66 We wanted people to hear the pavilion before they see it, and make it bang 99

Meneesha Kellay, curator (speaking of the soundtrack). Quoted in 'The Observer'

Angolan artist Sandra Poulson has used blue soap from Luanda to make sculptures of everyday objects
Photo by Marco Zorzanello. Courtesy La Biennale di Venezia

GREECE

EXHIBITION TITLE:

Bodies of water

CURATED BY:

Costis Paniyiris and Andreas Nikolovgenis

GIARDINI   MAP REF **[G]** P. **15**   *GIARDINI PLAN P. **12***

Venue: Giardini della Biennale, Castello
Vaporetto: Giardini; Giardini Biennale

⊙ The Greek pavilion showcases the transformative impact of dams and reservoirs in the country. These structures have significantly altered the arid landscape since the 1930s, creating a network of artificial lakes across the rugged terrain. This extensive water retention program serves multiple purposes, including irrigation, water supply, and energy generation. The exhibition highlights how these public architectural projects represent a collective effort for the well-being and progress of the community, providing essential resources and reflecting the pride and dedication of its inhabitants. It also acknowledges the problematic presence of these grand technical works as a new hydro-geological map of the country is invented.

⊕ COMMISSIONER: Efthimios Bakoyannis, Secretary General of Territorial Planning and Urban Environment

VISITING

DATES: 20 May–26 Nov 2023

HOURS: 20 May–30 Sep: Tue–Sun 11:00–19:00. 1 Oct–26 Nov: Tue–Sun 10:00–18:00. Last entry 15 mins before closing

CLOSED: Mon (except 22 May, 14 Aug, 4 Sep, 16 Oct, 30 Oct, 20 Nov)

ADMISSION: Biennale ticket. Available online only. See p. 9 for full details

TICKET INFO: labiennale. org/en/architecture/2023/ information#tickets

❝ **The Greek participation presents dams and reservoirs that transform the country ... as proud distillations of collective toil and concern for progress** ❞
Curatorial statement

The shape of water – namely Pigon Aoou, capacity 180,000,000m³
Photo by Matteo de Mayda. Courtesy La Biennale di Venezia

GRENADA

EXHIBITION TITLE:
Walking on Water

CURATED BY:
Luisa Flora

EXHIBITORS:
The Crew: Alexis Andrews, Alwyn Enoe, Asher Mains, Associazione Vela al Terzo members, Everton Peters, Fredericka Adam, James Douglas, Massimo Marchiori (aka Stari Rìbar), Melinda Hughes, Sarah Baker. The Flotilla: contributors from Barbados, China, Dominican Republic, Grenada

CITY MAP REF **[N/5]** P. **14–15**

Venue: Associazione Vela al Terzo Venezia, Fondamenta Calle Giazzo, Castello 209
Vaporetto: Bacini – Arsenale Nord

> The show's title refers to the challenges faced by both the people of Venice and Grenada due to climate change, and focuses on traditional Grenadian wooden boat construction and use. It includes a flotilla of 'Little Boats' made of various unlikely materials; the film 'Vanishing Sails', documenting wooden boats built in Grenada and Venice, which is projected onto recycled sails; art made from Venice's discarded plastic; and an essay on the development of wooden boat building.

grenadavenice.org

COMMISSIONER: Susan Mains, Ministry of Culture

VISITING

DATES: 20 May–26 Nov 2023
HOURS: 20 May–30 Sep: Tue–Sun 11:00–19:00. 1 Oct–26 Nov: Tue–Sun 10:00–18:00
CLOSED: Mon (except 22 May, 14 Aug, 4 Sep, 16 Oct, 30 Oct, 20 Nov)
ADMISSION: Free

66 By the very history of the island, the activity of building boats has its roots in the confluence of knowledge and memories from different origins 99

Curatorial statement

A traditional wooden boat in Grenada
Photo courtesy Grenada Arts Council 2023

HOLY SEE

EXHIBITION TITLE:

Social Friendship: meeting in the garden

CURATED BY:

Roberto Cremascoli

EXHIBITORS:
Álvaro Siza, Studio Albori (Emanuele Almagioni, Giacomo Borella, Fancesca Riva)

CITY MAP REF **[N/6]** P. **14–15**

Venue: Abbazia di San Giorgio Maggiore, Isola di San Giorgio Maggiore
Vaporetto: San Giorgio

⊙ The Vatican's pavilion is dedicated to social friendship, and invites visitors to care for the planet and celebrate the culture of encounter. Housed within the Benedictine Abbey, the exhibition unfolds from the entrance halls to the long gallery. Álvaro Siza's installation, 'O Encontro', leads visitors to the gardens, which have a new layout by Studio Albori. This shared space, normally reserved for the Benedictine community, will for the duration welcome outsiders, emphasizing dialogue and contemplation amidst vegetable patches and a chicken coop.

⊕ COMMISSIONER: Cardinale José Tolentino de Mendonça, Prefect of the Dicastery for Culture and Education of the Holy See

VISITING

DATES: 20 May–26 Nov 2023
HOURS: 20 May–30 Sep: Tue–Sun 11:00–19:00. 1 Oct–26 Nov: Tue–Sun 10:00–18:00
CLOSED: Mon (except 22 May, 14 Aug, 4 Sep, 16 Oct, 30 Oct, 20 Nov)
ADMISSION: Free
VISITING TIP: Elsewhere in the San Giorgio complex is a large Lego art installation by Ai Weiwei, open until 18 June 2023

❝ Over the 10 years of his pontificate Pope Francis has acted and spoken on involving all, without forgetting the peripheries, the poor and refugees ❞

Cardinal José Tolentino de Mendonca, Commissioner

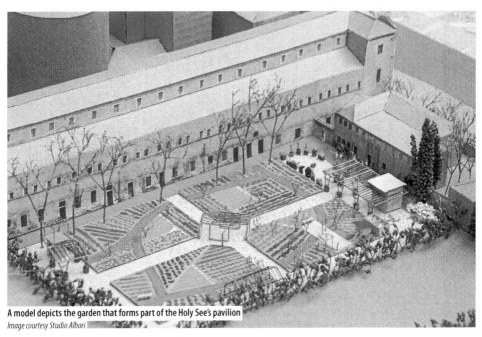

A model depicts the garden that forms part of the Holy See's pavilion
Image courtesy Studio Albori

HUNGARY

EXHIBITION TITLE:

Reziduum – The Frequency of Architecture

CURATED BY:

Mária Kondor-Szilágyi

EXHIBITORS:
Marcel Ferencz, Péter Mátrai, Judit Z. Halmágyi, Ferenc Haász

GIARDINI   MAP REF **[G]** P. **15**   *GIARDINI PLAN P.* ***12***

Venue: Giardini della Biennale, Castello
Vaporetto: Giardini; Giardini Biennale

➲ Focuses on the Museum of Ethnography in Budapest, designed by Marcel Ferencz. This unique museum has a rooftop garden, and a stunning metal shading lattice on the facade with patterns representing various cultures. In the pavilion, visitors can explore this ornamental lattice under special lighting. The multi-media experience continues with 'Soundcylinder', an innovative musical instrument; and an interactive computer program called 'MotifCreator', that enables users to create their own motifs using ornaments from the museum's collection.

reziduum.ludwigmuseum.hu/en

➕ COMMISSIONER: Julia Fabényi, director Ludwig Museum – Museum of Contemporary Art, Budapest

VISITING

DATES: 20 May–26 Nov 2023

HOURS: 20 May–30 Sep: Tue–Sun 11:00–19:00. 1 Oct–26 Nov: Tue–Sun 10:00–18:00. Last entry 15 mins before closing

CLOSED: Mon (except 22 May, 14 Aug, 4 Sep, 16 Oct, 30 Oct, 20 Nov)

ADMISSION: Biennale ticket. Available online only. See p. 9 for full details

TICKET INFO: labiennale. org/en/architecture/2023/ information#tickets

❝ **We aim to create a representation of a cultural memory where the different ethnological layers become visible** ❞

Curatorial statement

A close look at the Museum of Ethnography's ornamental lattice
Photo by Matteo de Mayda. Courtesy La Biennale di Venezia

IRELAND

EXHIBITION TITLE:

In Search of Hy-Brasil

CURATED BY:

Peter Cody, Peter Carroll, Elizabeth Hatz, Mary Laheen and Joseph Mackey

EXHIBITOR:
Hy-Brasil

ARSENALE   MAP REF **[A]** P. **15**   *ARSENALE PLAN P. 13*

Venue: Arsenale, Castello
Vaporetto: Arsenale

➲ The exhibition proposes the mythical Atlantic island of Hy-Brasil as a way to reimagine Ireland and its ocean territory. The curators have studied the cultures of Ireland's remote islands, focusing on Inis Meáin, Sceilg Mhicíl, and Cliara. Employing drawing, film, sound, and mapping, they create an immersive experience that highlights connections between social fabric, cultural landscape, and ecology. The installation uses natural light to mimic the islands' conditions, and incorporates large limestone slabs and tactile elements. It emphasizes the islands' sustainable livelihood practices, raising awareness about renewable energy, ethical food production, and biodiversity.

⊕ COMMISSIONER: Culture Ireland

VISITING

DATES: 20 May–26 Nov 2023
HOURS: 20 May–30 Sep: Tue, Wed, Thu, Sun 11:00–19:00; Fri, Sat, 11:00–20:00. 1 Oct–26 Nov: Tue–Sun 10:00–18:00. Last entry 15 mins before closing

CLOSED: Mon (except 22 May, 14 Aug, 4 Sep, 16 Oct, 30 Oct, 20 Nov)

ADMISSION: Biennale ticket. Available online only. See p. 9 for full details

TICKET INFO: labiennale. org/en/architecture/2023/ information#tickets

66 **Geographically remote and mainly peripheral to contemporary discourse, our islands are by necessity robust, resilient and inventive places** 99

Curatorial statement

An environment conjuring the mythical Atlantic island of Hy-Brasil
Photo by Andrea Avezzù. Courtesy La Biennale di Venezia

ISRAEL

EXHIBITION TITLE:

Cloud-to-Ground

CURATED BY:

Oren Eldar, Edith Kofsky, Hadas Maor

EXHIBITORS:

Oren Eldar, Edith Kofsky, Daniel Meir

GIARDINI   MAP REF **[G]** P. **15**   *GIARDINI PLAN P.* **12**

Venue: Giardini della Biennale, Castello
Vaporetto: Giardini; Giardini Biennale

❯ In scientific terminology, lightning can be called a 'cloud-to-ground' occurrence. Israel uses this phrase as a springboard to examine modern communication networks in Israel and its surroundings, namely digital data (cloud) and terrestrial storage and transmission infrastructures (ground).Their show looks at the fast-paced changes happening in these information infrastructures, and how architecture plays a role. The pavilion includes an immersive installation of abstract concrete maquettes, evoking the transition from analog to digital and from accessible buildings in urban hotspots to sealed structures in peripheral locations. Or – as the curators describe it – 'the hardware of the Fourth Industrial Revolution'.

✚ COMMISSIONER: Michael Gov, Arad Turgeman

VISITING

DATES: 20 May–26 Nov 2023

HOURS: 20 May–30 Sep: Tue–Sun 11:00–19:00. 1 Oct–26 Nov: Tue–Sun 10:00–18:00. Last entry 15 mins before closing

CLOSED: Mon (except 22 May, 14 Aug, 4 Sep, 16 Oct, 30 Oct, 20 Nov)

ADMISSION: Biennale ticket. Available online only. See p. 9 for full details

TICKET INFO: labiennale. org/en/architecture/2023/information#tickets

❝ **By surveying … these information infrastructures, the exhibition highlights the economic and geopolitical processes currently underway in Israel and the region** ❞

Curatorial statement

Abstract concrete maquettes line the pavilion's courtyard
Photo by Matteo de Mayda. Courtesy La Biennale di Venezia

ITALY

EXHIBITION TITLE:

Spaziale: Everyone Belongs to Everyone Else

CURATED BY:

Fosbury Architecture (F.A.)

INVITED PRACTICES:

(ab)Normal, BB, Captcha Architecture, Giuditta Vendrame, HPO, Lemonot, Orizzontale, Parasite 2.0, Post Disaster, Studio Ossidiana

ARSENALE   MAP REF **[A]** P. **15**   *ARSENALE PLAN P.* ***13***

Venue: Arsenale, Castello
Vaporetto: Arsenale

➲ An exhibition focused on community engagement. Rather than showcasing completed projects, it serves as a platform for projects led by young Italian architects, connected to specific communities across the country. The participating firms collaborate with artists, performers, food system specialists, AI experts, and more, to create interdisciplinary solutions. Examples include democratizing recreational activities in Venice, and promoting sustainable food systems in Sardinia.

spaziale2023.it/en

➕ COMMISSIONER: Onofrio Cutaia, General Directorate of Contemporary Creativity, Ministry of Culture

VISITING

DATES: 20 May–26 Nov 2023

HOURS: 20 May–30 Sep: Tue, Wed, Thu, Sun 11:00–19:00; Fri, Sat, 11:00–20:00. 1 Oct–26 Nov: Tue–Sun 10:00–18:00. Last entry 15 mins before closing

CLOSED: Mon (except 22 May, 14 Aug, 4 Sep, 16 Oct, 30 Oct, 20 Nov)

ADMISSION: Biennale ticket. Available online only. See p. 9 for full details

TICKET INFO: labiennale. org/en/architecture/2023/ information#tickets

❝ **The nine projects will shape the stages of a new geography, becoming symbolic destinations of a renewed Italian journey** ❞

Curatorial statement

One of many intriguing installations to be found in this wide-ranging exhibition
Photo by Marco Zorzanello. Courtesy La Biennale di Venezia

JAPAN

EXHIBITION TITLE:

Architecture, a place to be loved – when architecture is seen as a living creature

CURATED BY:

Onishi Maki

EXHIBITORS:

Hyakuda Yuki, Tada Tomomi, Harada Yuma, dot architects (Ienari Toshikatsu, Doi Wataru, Ikeda Ai, Miyachi Keiko), Moriyama Akane, Mizuno Futoshi

GIARDINI MAP REF **[G]** P. **15**   *GIARDINI PLAN P. 12*

Venue: Giardini della Biennale, Castello
Vaporetto: Giardini; Giardini Biennale

➲ This year, the Japan Pavilion celebrates itself – an architectural delight designed by Takamasa Yoshizaka (1917–1980), who studied under Le Corbusier and Wajiro Kon. Here, his lightly floating pavilion has undergone temporary interventions that highlight its modernist essence, including a tent roof, hanging mobiles, animated projections, and a rest area amid the piloti. Works on display cover such diverse fields as textiles, ceramics, design, metalwork, and animation. The pavilion is also hosting talks, workshops, and events to maintain its 50-year status as a vibrant and cherished space.

➕ COMMISSIONER: The Japan Foundation

VISITING

DATES: 20 May–26 Nov 2023

HOURS: 20 May–30 Sep: Tue–Sun 11:00–19:00. 1 Oct–26 Nov: Tue–Sun 10:00–18:00. Last entry 15 mins before closing

CLOSED: Mon (except 22 May, 14 Aug, 4 Sep, 16 Oct, 30 Oct, 20 Nov)

ADMISSION: Biennale ticket. Available online only. See p. 9 for full details

TICKET INFO: labiennale. org/en/architecture/2023/information#tickets

❝ Creating something involves giving it life ❞

Takamasa Yoshizaka, architect of the pavilion

❝ It is interesting to wonder how our gaze would change if the Japan Pavilion were a living creature ❞

Onishi Maki, curator

A temporary tent roof is suspended from building's facade
Photo by Matteo de Mayda. Courtesy La Biennale di Venezia

KOREA *(Republic of)*

EXHIBITION TITLE:

2086: Together How?

CURATED BY:

Soik Jung, Kyong Park

EXHIBITORS:

Soik Jung, Kyong Park , Soik Jung, Kyong Park, Yehre Suh (Urban Terrains Lab, UTL) x WoonGi Min, Yerin Kang (Seoul National University), Lee Chi-hoon (SoA) x Zoosun Yoon (Chungnam National University, UDTT lab.), Ahram Chae (Studio UDTT), Nahyun Hwang, David Eugin Moon (N H D M) x Wolsik Kim, Jaekyung Jung, Sunhee Yang (Gute form), Chris Ro (A Dear Friend), OUR LABOUR

GIARDINI MAP REF **[G]** P. **15** *GIARDINI PLAN P.* **12**

Venue: Giardini della Biennale, Castello
Vaporetto: Giardini; Giardini Biennale

➲ In the year 2086, the global population is projected to peak. This show looks at how people can collaborate and endure current and future environmental crises, focusing on that year. It is based around a quiz show-style game called 'The Game of Together How', that asks visitors multiple-choice questions regarding the choices they may have to make to survive. It also presents three collaborative projects by architects and community leaders around population increase and decline.

korean-pavilion.or.kr

➕ COMMISSIONER: Arts Council Korea

VISITING

DATES: 20 May–26 Nov 2023

HOURS: 20 May–30 Sep: Tue–Sun 11:00–19:00. 1 Oct–26 Nov: Tue–Sun 10:00–18:00. Last entry 15 mins before closing

CLOSED: Mon (except 22 May, 14 Aug, 4 Sep, 16 Oct, 30 Oct, 20 Nov)

ADMISSION: Biennale ticket. Available online only. See p. 9 for full details

TICKET INFO: labiennale. org/en/architecture/2023/ information#tickets

❝ Why are we so insecure about our future when so many of us are living at unprecedented levels of wealth, consumption, and freedom? ❞

The curators. Quoted in 'Dezeen'

A quiz show-style game asks visitors how they would survive environmental crisis
Photo by Matteo de Mayda. Courtesy La Biennale di Venezia

KOSOVO *(Republic of)*

EXHIBITION TITLE:
rks² transcendent locality

CURATED BY:
Dafina Morina

EXHIBITORS:
Poliksen Qorri-Dragaj, Hamdi Qorri

ARSENALE MAP REF **[A]** P. **15**   *ARSENALE PLAN P.* **13**

Venue: Arsenale, Castello
Vaporetto: Arsenale

➡ Kosovo explores translocality, a form of migration where individuals live in multiple places simultaneously, maintaining connections between their homeland and host land. The show examines the impact of this migration on Kosovar cities and urban planning – starting with the conflict faced by marginalized Albanians in the late 1980s, an event which led to mass migration. The installation is made up of modules that represent memories from the homeland and new experiences from the host land. An abstract house hangs upside-down from the roof; its metal frames symbolize formal borders, while neon tubes evoke the diaspora, and feeling of being in-between.

pavilionofkosovo.com

➕ COMMISSIONER: Dafina Morina

VISITING
DATES: 20 May–26 Nov 2023

HOURS: 20 May–30 Sep: Tue, Wed, Thu, Sun 11:00–19:00; Fri, Sat, 11:00–20:00. 1 Oct–26 Nov: Tue–Sun 10:00–18:00. Last entry 15 mins before closing

CLOSED: Mon (except 22 May, 14 Aug, 4 Sep, 16 Oct, 30 Oct, 20 Nov)

ADMISSION: Biennale ticket. Available online only. See p. 9 for full details

TICKET INFO: labiennale. org/en/architecture/2023/ information#tickets

> 66 **Up to the present day, migration plays a significant role in the social development of Kosovo … The exhibition deals with a special form of migration** 99
>
> *Curatorial statement*

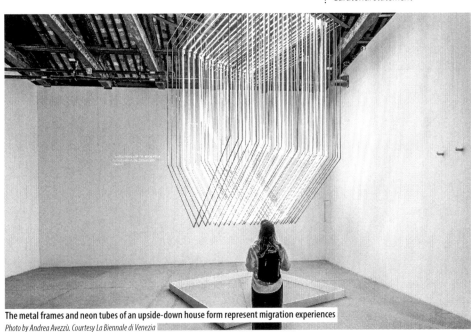

The metal frames and neon tubes of an upside-down house form represent migration experiences
Photo by Andrea Avezzù. Courtesy La Biennale di Venezia

KUWAIT

EXHIBITION TITLE:

Rethinking Rethinking Kuwait

CURATED BY:

Hamad Alkhaleefi, Naser Ashour, Mohammad Kassem, Rabab Raes Kazem

EXHIBITORS:

Abdulaziz Bazuhair, Abdullah Albusaili, Abdulrahman Sadeq, Aliaa Mahdy, Aziz Motawa, Bader Al Moulah, Batool Ashour, Dana Alrashid, Fareed Alghimlas, Fatima Al Fulaij, Hasan Al Saffar, Jassim Alelwani, Jassim Alnashmi, Latifa Al-Hajji, Maha Al Asaker, Malak Al Suwaihel, Maryam Mohammed, Mohammed Khesroh, Nada Abu-Daqer, Noor Abdulkhaleq, Nour Jafar, Nourah Alazmi, Qutaiba Buyabes, Sara Al-zeer, Sayer Al Sayer, Suad Al-Bahar, Sultan Alsamhan, Vinod Kumar, Yasmeen Abdal, Zahra Al-Mahdi, Zahra Hashim

CITY MAP REF **[N/7]** P. **14–15**

Venue: Magazzino del Sale 5, Fondamenta Zattere ai Saloni, Dorsoduro 262
Vaporetto: Spirito Santo

➲ This exhibition examines how modern urban planning in Kuwait erased much of its historic architecture, and how we can learn from this to shape future developments by considering decarbonization and decolonization. It includes diverse studies of transitional spaces in Kuwait City and the wider nation.

➕ COMMISSIONER: Abdulaziz Al-Mazeedi, National Council for Culture Arts and Literature / Kuwait (NCCAL)

VISITING

DATES: 20 May–26 Nov 2023
HOURS: 20 May–30 Sep: Tue–Sun 11:00–19:00. 1 Oct–26 Nov: Tue–Sun 10:00–18:00
CLOSED: Mon (except 22 May, 14 Aug, 4 Sep, 16 Oct, 30 Oct, 20 Nov)
ADMISSION: Free

❝ **The walled city of Kuwait, once the home of numerous aspects of Kuwaiti civil life, was mostly eradicated to make way for modernisation ... Large roads now cut through its history** ❞

Curatorial statement

'Envisioning the Future of Kuwait', 2023, a collage by Rabab Raes Kazem that imagines an elevated transportation system within the existing urban fabric
Image © Rabab Raes Kazem. Courtesy Pavilion of Kuwait

LATVIA

EXHIBITION TITLE:
T/C Latvija (TCL)

CURATED BY:
Ernests Cerbulis, Uldis Jaunzems-Pētersons

EXHIBITORS:
Ints Meņģelis, Toms Kampars

ARSENALE MAP REF **[A]** P. **15**   *ARSENALE PLAN P. 13*

Venue: Arsenale, Castello
Vaporetto: Arsenale

➲ The Latvian team gives an entertaining twist to the Biennale format. With the help of AI, they have transformed over 500 pavilions from past architecture biennales into packaged products displayed in a mini-mart-like setting. Visitors are invited to browse the garish wares, using shopping carts and a checkout, mimicking the overwhelming experience of trying to see all the pavilions in one visit. It's a playful critique, raising the question of whether the biennale has become too bloated. The 'shop' offers concepts from the last 10 biennales, emphasizing the role of choice and commercial dynamics in architecture.

latvianpavilion.lv

➊ COMMISSIONER: Jānis Dripe, Ministry of Culture of the Republic of Latvia

VISITING
DATES: 20 May–26 Nov 2023

HOURS: 20 May–30 Sep: Tue, Wed, Thu, Sun 11:00–19:00; Fri, Sat, 11:00–20:00. 1 Oct–26 Nov: Tue–Sun 10:00–18:00. Last entry 15 mins before closing

CLOSED: Mon (except 22 May, 14 Aug, 4 Sep, 16 Oct, 30 Oct, 20 Nov)

ADMISSION: Biennale ticket. Available online only. See p. 9 for full details

TICKET INFO: labiennale. org/en/architecture/2023/ information#tickets

> **❝ The department store is more than just a shopping centre, it is a data system … its success is dependent on quality of the information and data it collects ❞**
>
> *Ernests Cerbulis. From essay 'Supermarkets As Future Laboratories'*

Shopping for concepts with Latvia
Photo by Andrea Avezzù. Courtesy La Biennale di Venezia

LITHUANIA

EXHIBITION TITLE:
Children's Forest Pavilion

CURATED BY:
Jurga Daubaraitė, Egija Inzule, Jonas Žukauskas

EXHIBITORS:
Aistė Ambrazevičiūtė, Gabrielė Grigorjeva, Laura Garbštienė, Mantas Petraitis, Monika Janulevičiūtė, Kornelija Žalpytė, Jonas Žukauskas, Antanas Gerlikas, Jurgis Paškevičius, Anton Shramkov, Ignė Narbutaitė, Elis Hannikainen, Eitvydas Doškus, Nomeda and Gediminas Urbonas / Urbonas Studio, Kristupas Sabolius / School of Creativity, Nene Tsuboi and Tuomas Toivonen / New Academy, Tiina Arjukka Hirvonen, Michaela Casková, Robin Everett, Riitta Nykänen / Mustarinda Association, Ancient Woods Foundation

CITY MAP REF **[N/8]** P. **14-15**

Venue: Campo della Tana (entrance in Ramo della Tana), Castello 2125
Vaporetto: Arsenale

➲ This pavilion is designed as a playscape for youngsters to learn about forests. It displays the results of outdoor activities with children in Lithuanian and Finnish woodlands, instilling the idea of forests as shared spaces. Subjects studied include ancient forests, swamp landscapes, lichens, pollution, and ecosystem resilience. The construction uses timber from trees grown in the native woodlands of the Curonian Spit. After the show it will be returned there, and used for educational workshops.

➕ COMMISSIONER: Ines Weizman

VISITING

DATES: 20 May–26 Nov 2023
HOURS: 20 May–30 Sep: Tue–Sun 11:00–19:00. 1 Oct–26 Nov: Tue–Sun 10:00–18:00
CLOSED: Mon (except 22 May, 14 Aug, 4 Sep, 16 Oct, 30 Oct, 20 Nov)
ADMISSION: Free

❝ **The main role in developing and curating this installation is given to a collaboration with children and young adults as consultants, allies and the pavilion's ideal audience** ❞

Curatorial statement

Playing with 'Mountain Pine Alphabet', a piece by Mantas Peteraitis
Photo by Rasa Juškevičiūtė. Courtesy Pavilion of Lithuania

MEXICO

EXHIBITION TITLE:

Infraestructura utópica: La cancha de básquetbol campesina / Utopian Infrastructure: The Campesino Basketball Court

CURATORS / EXHIBITORS:

APRDELESP and Mariana Botey

ARSENALE MAP REF **[A]** P. **15**   *ARSENALE PLAN P. 13*

Venue: Arsenale, Castello
Vaporetto: Arsenale

⮕ Mexico recreates a vibrant, life-sized fragment of a 'campesino' basketball court – *campesino* being a broad term for members of the Latin American rural working class. Very different from their USA counterparts, these infrastructures represent a decolonized meeting place for indigenous communities, serving as a temporary social space for various activities like playing, debating, working, and hanging out. Beyond its sports theme, the *campesino* court symbolizes creativity, enjoyment, and dialogue within both urban and rural settings. Adjacent to it is a socializing area for music and dance, creating a smart, entertaining, and well-coordinated experience.

➕ COMMISSIONER: Diego E. Sapién Muñoz, National Institute of Fine Arts and Literature

VISITING

DATES: 20 May–26 Nov 2023

HOURS: 20 May–30 Sep: Tue, Wed, Thu, Sun 11:00–19:00; Fri, Sat, 11:00–20:00. 1 Oct–26 Nov: Tue–Sun 10:00–18:00. Last entry 15 mins before closing

CLOSED: Mon (except 22 May, 14 Aug, 4 Sep, 16 Oct, 30 Oct, 20 Nov)

ADMISSION: Biennale ticket. Available online only. See p. 9 for full details

TICKET INFO: labiennale. org/en/architecture/2023/ information#tickets

❝ The concept is based on the scheme of a basketball court as a research laboratory … creativity, fun and dialogue in a recognized space in urban and rural environments ❞

Curatorial statement

The pavilion presents a life-sized fragment of a Mexican basketball court

Photo by Marco Zorzanello. Courtesy La Biennale di Venezia

MONTENEGRO

EXHIBITION TITLE:
Mirages of the Future (MNE)

CURATED BY:
Zoran Lazovic

EXHIBITORS:
Ninoslav Mitrić, Branislav Milatović, Andrija Mugoša, Duško Miljanić, Branislav Strugar, Lazar Pejović, Maja Žugić, Vlado Lutovac, Marko Stjepčević, Marko Radonjić, Radovan Radoman, Eldin Kabaklija, Jovana Marojević and Milica Jaramaz, Darko Radović, Davisi Boontharm and co+re.team, Mileta Bojović, Luka Skansi, Djordje Stojanovic, Milan Katic and Milica Vujovic, Petra Čoko, Rok Žnidaršič, Goran Ivo Marinovic, Nikola Novaković, Marija Novaković, Srđan Marlović, Bratislav Braca Gaković, Mustafa Musić, Anoe Melliou, Artem Terteryan, Zlatko Nikolic, Mladen Maslovar, Anđelka Bnin-Bninski, Srdjan Tadić, Jelena Vlaović, Aleksandra Saša Vukićević, Anja Tadić, Bojan Vlahović and Aleksandar Marsenić, Milena Delević Grbić, Darko Karadjitch, Aleksandar Čarnojević, Aleksandar Suhanov and Marijana Simić, Jelena Ivančević, Ana Tošić, Sara Jeveričić, Đurđa Garčević, Andrej Jovanović, Ema Alihodžić, Jašarović Nemanja Milićević, Goran Andrejin and Sonja Dubak, Maša Mušikić, Andjelka Bnin-Bninski, Stanislava Predojević and Ksenija Radovanović

CITY MAP REF **[N/9]** P. **14–15**

Venue: Palazzo Malipiero, Ramo Malipiero (off Campo San Samuele), San Marco 3078–3079/A
Vaporetto: San Samuele

⊘ Over 150 works by many creators, which use Montenegro's wealth of natural resources, and rich cultural heritage, as a context within which to explore new ideas for the future.
mirages.me

⊕ COMMISSIONER: Vladan Stevović

VISITING

DATES: 20 May–26 Nov 2023
HOURS: 20 May–30 Sep: Tue–Sun 11:00–19:00. 1 Oct–26 Nov: Tue–Sun 10:00–18:00
CLOSED: Mon (except 22 May, 14 Aug, 4 Sep, 16 Oct, 30 Oct, 20 Nov)
ADMISSION: Free

❝ **The aim of the exhibition is to encourage qualitative changes in the natural, urban and protected environment** ❞
Curatorial statement

A view of Kotor city and bay in Montenegro
Photo by Geotiger18, Wikimedia Commons

NETHERLANDS *(The)*

EXHIBITION TITLE:
Plumbing the System

CURATED BY:
Jan Jongert / Superuse

EXHIBITOR:
Carlijn Kingma in collaboration with Thomas Bollen, Martijn Jeroen van der Linden, an Jongert, Frank Feder, Valentina Cella, Junyuann Chen, Césare Peeren / (Superuse), Marit Janse (De Urbanisten) in collaboration with Friso Klapwijk (Wavin) and Afrikaander Wijkcooperatie Rotterdam

GIARDINI   MAP REF **[G]** P. **15**   *GIARDINI PLAN P.* **12**

Venue: Giardini della Biennale, Castello
Vaporetto: Giardini; Giardini Biennale

➲ Proposes a low-tech water retention system for the Dutch pavilion that captures enough rainfall to meet its own water needs, while also improving the surrounding Giardini. The show opens with architect Carlijn Kingma's vast collaborative drawing 'The Waterworks of Money', which illustrates the complex financial systems that underpin society. Water here is a metaphor for the need to rethink such systems. But can cultural events go beyond theoretical discussions, and actually address these urgent issues? To answer yes, the Dutch team will document the installation of its new water system, inspiring future change.

➕ COMMISSIONER: Aric Chen, Het Nieuwe Instituut

VISITING

DATES: 20 May–26 Nov 2023

HOURS: 20 May–30 Sep: Tue–Sun 11:00–19:00. 1 Oct–26 Nov: Tue–Sun 10:00–18:00. Last entry 15 mins before closing

CLOSED: Mon (except 22 May, 14 Aug, 4 Sep, 16 Oct, 30 Oct, 20 Nov)

ADMISSION: Biennale ticket. Available online only. See p. 9 for full details

TICKET INFO: labiennale. org/en/architecture/2023/ information#tickets

> ❝ **Just like money, water is a flow that runs from one point to another … By using water, the story of the economy can be explained to a larger audience** ❞
>
> *Jan Jongert, curator. Quoted in 'Parametric Architecture'*

Carlijn Kingma's large-scale metaphorical drawing, 'The Waterworks of Money'
Photo by Matteo de Mayda. Courtesy La Biennale di Venezia

NIGER *(Republic of)*

EXHIBITION TITLE:
Archifusion

CURATED BY:
Boris Brollo

ISLAND   MAP REF **[N/10]** P. **14–15**

Venue: San Servolo island, Isola di San Servolo
Vaporetto: San Servolo

○→ This is Niger's first time at an Architecture biennale, with their pavilion sited across the water from San Marco on the university island of San Servolo. Their presentation blends African and Western cultures to create a unique cultural laboratory. The project focuses on collaboration and the exchange of knowledge among all parties involved, overcoming barriers imposed by intellectual property rights. It introduces a modified brick called 'Brique Magique', intended to preserve Niger's architectural history while adding new decorative techniques. This brick allows for stronger walls, better insulation, and the possibility of incorporating local aggregates. Italian artists contribute by reinterpreting traditional house decorations in a modern context.

⊕ COMMISSIONER: Ibrahim Souleymane

VISITING
DATES: 20 May–26 Nov 2023
HOURS: Thu–Sat 11:00–17:00
CLOSED: Sun–Wed
ADMISSION: Free

❝ Intellectual property … creates additional barriers which exclude countries that are technologically less advanced. 'Archifusion' intends to overcome these barriers by placing the most advanced technologies at the service of a 'different' (mixed) culture ❞

Curatorial statement

Promotional image for the exhibition
Courtesy Pavilion of Republic of Niger

NORDIC COUNTRIES
(Norway, Finland, Sweden)

EXHIBITION TITLE:
Girjegumpi: The Sámi Architecture Library

CURATED BY:
Carlos Mínguez Carrasco and James Taylor-Foster (ArkDes)

EXHIBITOR:
Joar Nango

GIARDINI MAP REF **[G]** P. **15**   *GIARDINI PLAN P.* **12**

Venue: Giardini della Biennale, Castello
Vaporetto: Giardini; Giardini Biennale

◉ The much-praised Nordic presentation celebrates the nomadic Sámi culture across Norway, Sweden, and Finland. Led by artist-architect Joar Nango, it features his 20-year project 'Girjegumpi', a mobile hut on sledges that doubles as a library and social space. The pavilion houses a collection of crafts and techniques, including stitching, painting, carpentry, and reindeer and seal hides. It is a collaborative and inviting environment, filled with the aroma of timber and leather – a captivating way to explore the world of Sámi architecture and indigenous traditions.

⊕ COMMISSIONER: Kieran Long, ArkDes – The Swedish Centre for Architecture and Design; Stina Høgkvist, The National Museum of Norway; Carina Jaatinen, The Museum of Finnish Architecture

VISITING

DATES: 20 May–26 Nov 2023

HOURS: 20 May–30 Sep: Tue–Sun 11:00–19:00. 1 Oct–26 Nov: Tue–Sun 10:00–18:00. Last entry 15 mins before closing

CLOSED: Mon (except 22 May, 14 Aug, 4 Sep, 16 Oct, 30 Oct, 20 Nov)

ADMISSION: Biennale ticket. Available online only. See p. 9 for full details

TICKET INFO: labiennale. org/en/architecture/2023/ information#tickets

❝ **Sámi people are colonized people, but our lands are still being expropriated. Sámi architecture is something that we need to talk about** ❞

Joar Nango, exhibitor. Quoted in 'Dezeen'

The pavilion houses a collection of crafts and techniques
Photo by Matteo de Mayda. Courtesy La Biennale di Venezia

NORTH MACEDONIA
(Republic of)

EXHIBITION TITLE:

Stories of the Summer School of Architecture in the St. Joakim Osogovski Monastery 1992–2017

CURATED BY:

Ognen Marina, Dimitar Krsteski, Aleksandar Petanovski, Darko Draganovski, Marija Petrova, Gordan Petrov

EXHIBITORS:

Faculty of Architecture Ss Cyril and Methodius University in Skopje, Minas Bakalchev, Mitko Hadji Pulja, Aleksandar Radevski, Saša Tasić, Dimitar Papasterevski

CITY MAP REF **[N/11]** P. **14–15**

Venue: Scuola dei Laneri, Salizada San Pantalon, Santa Croce 131/A
Vaporetto: Piazzale Roma; San Tomà

➲ Dedicated to the Faculty of Architecture's summer school at the state university, and featuring elegiac work by several alumni, this show looks at the contrast between everyday reality and the grandeur of architecture. It considers elements such as houses, streets, districts, transitional prototypes, forgotten spaces, discarded materials, natural landscapes, hidden mazes, intersections – and a sense of belonging.

➕ COMMISSIONER: Dita Starova Kjerimi, National Gallery of Macedonia

VISITING

DATES: 20 May–26 Nov 2023

HOURS: 20 May–30 Sep: Tue–Sun 11:00–19:00. 1 Oct–26 Nov: Tue–Sun 10:00–18:00

CLOSED: Mon (except 22 May, 14 Aug, 4 Sep, 16 Oct, 30 Oct, 20 Nov)

ADMISSION: Free

❝ We want to establish a dynamic reconstruction of the work of many, through memories, recollections and stories ❞

Curatorial statement

The St. Joakim Osogovski Monastery, where the architecture summer school was held
Photo by MacedonianBoy, Wikimedia Commons

PANAMA *(Republic of)*

EXHIBITION TITLE:
Panama: Stories from beneath the water

CURATED BY:
Aimée Lam Tunon

EXHIBITORS:
Dante Furioso, Joan Flores-Villalobos, Danilo Pérez, Alejandro Pinto, Luis Pulido Ritter, Marixa Lasso

CITY MAP REF **[N/12]** P. **14–15**

Venue: Tana Art Space, Fondamenta de la Tana, Castello 2109/A and 2110–2111
Vaporetto: Arsenale

➲ Panama's Biennale debut examines the historical context of the former Panama Canal Zone, which was under US control in the early 20th century. It reveals stories of division and integration, referencing three examples: the divisive architectural structures, the submerged communities with erased identities, and the island of Barro Colorado, formed when the Chagres River was dammed to form a lake in 1913. An installation of blue lights attracts insects and projects their shadows on the walls, symbolizing the connection between the colonizer's perspective and Plato's allegory of the cave.

➕ COMMISSIONER: Itzela Quirós

VISITING

DATES: 20 May–26 Nov 2023
HOURS: Tue–Sun 11:00–18:00
CLOSED: Mon
ADMISSION: Free

❝ **Since ancient times, the tropics have been widely recognized as a symbol of exotic beauty … the exhibition should provide a counter-narrative to this, with Panama as a case study for a future vision of a 'tropical' nation** ❞

Aimée Lam Tunon, curator

A grid of blue lights, intended to attract insects
Courtesy Pavilion of Republic of Panama

PERU

EXHIBITION TITLE:
Walkers in Amazonia

CURATED BY:
Alexia León, Lucho Marcial

EXHIBITORS:
Waman Wasi et al

ARSENALE MAP REF **[A]** P. **15**   *ARSENALE PLAN P. 13*

Venue: Arsenale, Castello
Vaporetto: Arsenale

⊙ 'Walkers in Amazonia' focuses on millennia of care and maintenance in the Andean Amazonia region. Central to this is Waman Wasi's 'The Calendar Project', an audio-visual installation which allows visitors to connect their own cultural experiences with the everyday life of these territories. It represents a groundbreaking collaboration between the Peruvian government, 11 local education management units (UGEL), rural schools in San Martin, and various mestizo and native communities such as Kichwa Lamas, Shawi, and Awajún. By forging this alliance between schools and communities, the project nurtures a mutual exchange of knowledge about the diversity of tropical rainforests, fostering a new ecology of understanding and rejuvenation.

⊕ COMMISSIONER: José Orrego

VISITING

DATES: 20 May–26 Nov 2023

HOURS: 20 May–30 Sep: Tue, Wed, Thu, Sun 11:00–19:00; Fri, Sat, 11:00–20:00. 1 Oct–26 Nov: Tue–Sun 10:00–18:00. Last entry 15 mins before closing

CLOSED: Mon (except 22 May, 14 Aug, 4 Sep, 16 Oct, 30 Oct, 20 Nov)

ADMISSION: Biennale ticket. Available online only. See p. 9 for full details

TICKET INFO: labiennale. org/en/architecture/2023/ information#tickets

❝ **Imagine a new ecology of knowledge … cultivated through the practice of walking between regions** ❞

Curatorial statement

The entrance to the Peruvian pavilion
Photo by Marco Zorzanello. Courtesy La Biennale di Venezia

PHILIPPINES

EXHIBITION TITLE:
Tripa de Gallina: Guts of Estuary

CURATED BY:
Sam Domingo and Ar. Choie Y. Funk

EXHIBITORS:
The Architecture Collective – TAC (Bien M. Alvarez, Matthew S. Gan, Ar. Lyle D. La Madrid, and Arnold A. Rañada)

ARSENALE MAP REF **[A]** P. **15**   *ARSENALE PLAN P.* **13**

Venue: Arsenale, Castello
Vaporetto: Arsenale

⊙ Exposes the challenges faced by residents living along the sludgy estuary known as 'Tripa de Gallina' – 'guts of the rooster' – in three areas of Barangay. These locales have a dense population of informal settlers, leading to deleterious effects on the water's health. The exhibition highlights the dependence of Filipino communities on their waterways, and stresses the need for improved care. The curators propose a bamboo-made structure that serves as a space for meeting and discussion. By creating this space for the residents to gather, the curators hope to foster more collaboration on the issue.

⊕ COMMISSIONER: Victorino Mapa Manalo, Chairman National Commission for Culture and the Arts (NCCA)

VISITING

DATES: 20 May–26 Nov 2023

HOURS: 20 May–30 Sep: Tue, Wed, Thu, Sun 11:00–19:00; Fri, Sat, 11:00–20:00. 1 Oct–26 Nov: Tue–Sun 10:00–18:00. Last entry 15 mins before closing

CLOSED: Mon (except 22 May, 14 Aug, 4 Sep, 16 Oct, 30 Oct, 20 Nov)

ADMISSION: Biennale ticket. Available online only. See p. 9 for full details

TICKET INFO: labiennale. org/en/architecture/2023/ information#tickets

❝ **Just as murky as the waters are in the estuary, so are the settlers' relationships** ❞
Curatorial statement

An elegant bamboo-made structure intended to serve as a meeting space
Photo by Marco Zorzanello. Courtesy La Biennale di Venezia

POLAND

EXHIBITION TITLE:
Datament

CURATED BY:
Jacek Sosnowski

EXHIBITORS:
Anna Barlik, Marcin Strzała

GIARDINI   MAP REF **[G]** P. **15**   *GIARDINI PLAN P.* **12**

Venue: Giardini della Biennale, Castello
Vaporetto: Giardini; Giardini Biennale

➲ The title, 'Datament', is a neologism intended to convey the idea of the all-encompassing 'data establishment' that is constantly affecting our real world lives. The show offers visitors the chance to experience data in a physical form, via an installation of four life-size house frames occupying the pavilion. These structures faithfully replicate statistical data from four countries, literally depicting the impact of digital technologies on architecture and urban planning. By using averaged data on house shapes and layouts, the project challenges the reliance on processed information. It makes clear how relying solely on algorithmic data can lead to distorted and flawed outcomes.

labiennale.art.pl/en

➕ COMMISSIONER: Janusz Janowski

VISITING

DATES: 20 May–26 Nov 2023
HOURS: 20 May–30 Sep: Tue–Sun 11:00–19:00. 1 Oct–26 Nov: Tue–Sun 10:00–18:00. Last entry 15 mins before closing
CLOSED: Mon (except 22 May, 14 Aug, 4 Sep, 16 Oct, 30 Oct, 20 Nov)
ADMISSION: Biennale ticket. Available online only. See p. 9 for full details
TICKET INFO: labiennale. org/en/architecture/2023/ information#tickets

❝ **We let algorithms calculate and design our houses and cities. However, without a sensitive and conscious designer, digitally processed data can create distorted solutions** ❞

Curatorial statement

Colourful house-sized frames replicate statistical data from four countries
Photo by Matteo de Mayda. Courtesy La Biennale di Venezia

PORTUGAL

EXHIBITION TITLE:
Fertile Futures

CURATED BY:
Andreia Garcia

EXHIBITORS:
Álvaro Domingues, Ana Salgueiro, Aurora Carapinha, Corpo Atelier, Dulcineia Santos, Eglantina Monteiro, Érica Castanheira, Guida Marques, Ilhéu Atelier, João Mora Porteiro, João Pedro Matos Fernandes, Oficina Pedrêz, Ponto Atelier, Space Transcribers

CITY MAP REF **[N/13]** P. **14–15**

Venue: Palazzo Franchetti, Campiello San Vidal, San Marco 2847
Vaporetto: Accademia

➡ Focuses on water issues – or 'hydrogeographies' – in seven different areas of Portugal. Architects and experts from various fields collaborate on innovative approaches at the pavilion. The central hall is designed around a water line, symbolizing the flow of water. The dialogue extends beyond Venice with talks in Braga, Faro, and Porto Santo, as well as an international seminar in Fundão. The seminar includes workshops and installations to assist local communities in combating water scarcity.

fertilefutures.pt/en

➕ COMMISSIONER: Américo Rodrigues, General Directorate for the Arts

VISITING
DATES: 20 May–26 Nov 2023
HOURS: Tue–Sun 10:00–18:00
CLOSED: Mon (except 22 May, 14 Aug, 4 Sep, 16 Oct, 30 Oct, 20 Nov)
ADMISSION: Free

❝ **The title highlights the speculative nature of the Portuguese representation, intending to contribute to the design of futures that are more inclusive, equitable and diverse** ❞
Andreia Garcia, curator

Work mat during a study trip to the Douro, 2023
© *Dulcineia Santos Studio – Laboratório do Douro Internacional, 2023. Courtesy Pavilion of Portugal*

ROMANIA

EXHIBITION TITLE:

Now, Here, There

CURATED BY:

Emil Ivănescu, Simina Filat

EXHIBITORS:

Emil Ivănescu, Simina Filat, Catalin Berescu, Anca Maria Păsărin, National Technological Museum 'Prof. Eng. Dimitrie Leonida'

GIARDINI MAP REF **[G]** P. **15**   *GIARDINI PLAN P.* **12**

Venue: Giardini della Biennale, Castello

Vaporetto: Giardini; Giardini Biennale

CITY MAP REF **[N/14]** P. **14–15**

Venue: New Gallery of the Romanian Institute for Culture and Humanistic Research (aka Istituto Romeno di Cultura e Ricerca Umanistica), Palazzo Correr, Campo Santa Fosca, Cannaregio 2214

Vaporetto: San Marcuola

◑ A display of innovative early 20th-century Romanian inventions intended as creative inspiration. One stunner is an all-electric car built in 1904 that is still functional today. Other artefacts include the world's first aerodynamic car with all-wheel drive, and a social housing design created a century ago.

✚ COMMISSIONER: Attila Kim

VISITING

Giardini

DATES: 20 May–26 Nov 2023

HOURS: 20 May–30 Sep: Tue–Sun 11:00–19:00. 1 Oct–26 Nov: Tue–Sun 10:00–18:00. Last entry 15 mins before closing

CLOSED: Mon (except 22 May, 14 Aug, 4 Sep, 16 Oct, 30 Oct, 20 Nov)

ADMISSION: Biennale ticket. Available online only. See p. 9 for full details

TICKET INFO: labiennale. org/en/architecture/2023/ information#tickets

New Gallery of the Romanian Institute for Culture and Humanistic Research

DATES: 20 May–26 Nov 2023

HOURS: 20 May–30 Sep: Tue–Sun 11:00–19:00. 1 Oct–26 Nov: Tue–Sun 10:00–18:00

CLOSED: Mon (except 22 May, 14 Aug, 4 Sep, 16 Oct, 30 Oct, 20 Nov)

ADMISSION: Free

A group of innovative vintage cars forms a highlight of the display
Photo by Matteo de Mayda. Courtesy La Biennale di Venezia

SAN MARINO *(Republic of)*

EXHIBITION TITLE:
Ospite Ospitante

CURATED BY:
Michael Kaethler, Marco Pierini

EXHIBITORS:
Vittorio Corsini, students and teachers from: University of San Marino, Design and History; University of Bologna, Industrial Design; Stuttgart Technology University of Applied Sciences; Brera Academy of Fine Arts; Ca' Foscari University of Venice, Environmental Humanities; University of Applied Sciences Northwestern Switzerland, University of Art and Design, Industrial Design Institute; Order of Engineers and Architects of San Marino; Rotterdam University of Applied Sciences, Industrial Design Engineering; IUAV University of Venice, Industrial Design; University of Ferrara, Industrial Product Design

`CITY`   MAP REF **[N/15]** P. **14–15**

Venue: Calle San Lorenzo, Castello 5063/B
Vaporetto: Celestia; San Zaccaria

➲ A workshop on hospitality issues by artist Vittorio Corsini with a multitude of students. The show consists of two rooms: one for Corsini's artwork, providing a space for reflection, and another called 'Hospitality Lab', with activities based on the needs of the local population. Corsini has created three new works, including a plexiglass cube that responds to human presence.

➕ COMMISSIONER: Riccardo Varini

VISITING
DATES: 20 May–26 Nov 2023
HOURS: 20 May–30 Sep: Tue–Sun 11:00–19:00. 1 Oct–26 Nov: Tue–Sun 10:00–18:00
CLOSED: Mon (except 22 May, 14 Aug, 4 Sep, 16 Oct, 30 Oct, 20 Nov)
ADMISSION: Free

❝ We are all guests on this Earth, and yet we are also all hosts ❞
Curatorial statement

'Hospitality Lab', a rendering of the pavilion of the Republic of San Marino
Courtesy Pavilion of the Republic of San Marino

SAUDI ARABIA

EXHIBITION TITLE:

Irth ارث

CURATED BY:

Basma Bouzo, Noura Bouzo

EXHIBITORS:

Albara Osama Saimaldahar

ARSENALE MAP REF **[A]** P. **15**   *ARSENALE PLAN P. 13*

Venue: Arsenale, Castello
Vaporetto: Arsenale

○ This exhibition explores the qualities of materials in Saudi architecture, presented as an interactive journey. The project offers multiple perspectives for viewers to engage with and understand the fundamental components of local Saudi architecture. The Saudi team adopts a two-pronged strategy, focusing on the methodology of combining building components with innovative techniques, and showcasing the materiality of Saudi architecture in the present and future. Visitors are invited to participate in material investigation, contribute to a future legacy, and contemplate how past and present investigations can solve future challenges.

⊕ COMMISSIONER: Architecture and Design Commission, Ministry of Culture

VISITING

DATES: 20 May–26 Nov 2023

HOURS: 20 May–30 Sep: Tue, Wed, Thu, Sun 11:00–19:00; Fri, Sat, 11:00–20:00. 1 Oct–26 Nov: Tue–Sun 10:00–18:00. Last entry 15 mins before closing

CLOSED: Mon (except 22 May, 14 Aug, 4 Sep, 16 Oct, 30 Oct, 20 Nov)

ADMISSION: Biennale ticket. Available online only. See p. 9 for full details

TICKET INFO: labiennale. org/en/architecture/2023/ information#tickets

❝ Irth is a transliteration of the Arabic word that can either mean 'legacy' or 'treasured possession,' which encapsulates the intent of our curatorial vision ❞

Curatorial statement

The pavilion features beautiful modern interpretations of traditional Saudi forms
Photo by Marco Zorzanello. Courtesy La Biennale di Venezia

SERBIA

EXHIBITION TITLE:

In Reflections. 6°27'48.81"N 3°14'49.20"E

SCIENTIFIC COMMITTEE:

Biljana Jotić (President), Dubravka Đukanović, Jelena Ivanović Vojvodić, Miljana Zeković, Snežana Vesnić, Ana Đurić, Jelena Mitrović

EXHIBITORS:
Iva Njunjić, Tihomir Dičić

GIARDINI MAP REF **[G]** P. **15**   *GIARDINI PLAN P.* **12**

Venue: Giardini della Biennale, Castello
Vaporetto: Giardini; Giardini Biennale

⊙ Explores the impact of the Non-Aligned Movement and Yugoslav architects in transforming African cities during the 20th century. The exhibition revisits the International Fair in Lagos, built between 1974 and 1976, which involved the urbanization of 350 hectares of wetlands. It examines the fair's historical context, its role as a city project and architectural scheme, and its significance in shaping personal and collective consciousness. Through a time-space map, archival drawings, and travel videos, the exhibition presents the architectural identity of the fair and its relevance for the future.

⊕ COMMISSIONER: Slobodan Jović

VISITING

DATES: 20 May–26 Nov 2023

HOURS: 20 May–30 Sep: Tue–Sun 11:00–19:00. 1 Oct–26 Nov: Tue–Sun 10:00–18:00. Last entry 15 mins before closing

CLOSED: Mon (except 22 May, 14 Aug, 4 Sep, 16 Oct, 30 Oct, 20 Nov)

ADMISSION: Biennale ticket. Available online only. See p. 9 for full details

TICKET INFO: labiennale.org/en/architecture/2023/information#tickets

❝ The Lagos International Fair was once a destination for visitors to the World's Fair, and today it is a place that the city is pressing down with the weight of a growing demographic structure ❞

Curatorial statement

Detail of 'Southeast pavilion of The Trade Fair Complex in Lagos', 2023, by Tolulope Fatunbi
Photography © Tolulope Fatunbi. Private Collection. Courtesy Pavilion of Serbia

SINGAPORE

EXHIBITION TITLE:

When Is Enough, Enough?
The Performance of Measurement

CURATED BY:

Melvin Tan, Adrian Lai, Wong Ker How

EXHIBITORS:

Aurelia Chan, Elwin Chan, Zachary Chan, Kar-men Cheng Chew Yunqing, Lip Chiong, Aaron Choo, Calvin Chua, Joshua Adam Comaroff, Yann Follain, Srilalitha Gopalakrishnan, Richard Hassell, Hwang Yun-Hye, Anuj Jain,Emi Kiyota, Pennie Kwan, Bjorn Low, Jerome Ng Xin Hao, Isabella Ong, Ong Ker-Shing, Firdaus Sani, Thomas Schroepfer, Annabelle Tan, Wong Chun Sing, Mun Summ Wong

ARSENALE MAP REF **[A]** P. **15**   *ARSENALE PLAN P. 13*

Venue: Arsenale, Castello
Vaporetto: Arsenale

➲ Based around a giant analog plotter dubbed the 'Values Measurement Machine', whose towering calligraphic scrolls record the response of visitors to questions about the qualities of their ideal habitat. Around this are displayed projects dealing with issues ranging from neurodiversity to rewilding.

singaporepavilion.sg

➕ COMMISSIONER: Yap Lay Bee, Group Director (Architecture & Urban Design), Urban Redevelopment Authority; Dawn Lim, Executive Director, DesignSingapore Council

VISITING

DATES: 20 May–26 Nov 2023

HOURS: 20 May–30 Sep: Tue, Wed, Thu, Sun 11:00–19:00; Fri, Sat, 11:00–20:00. 1 Oct–26 Nov: Tue–Sun 10:00–18:00. Last entry 15 mins before closing

CLOSED: Mon (except 22 May, 14 Aug, 4 Sep, 16 Oct, 30 Oct, 20 Nov)

ADMISSION: Biennale ticket. Available online only. See p. 9 for full details

TICKET INFO: labiennale. org/en/architecture/2023/ information#tickets

❝ **Navigating through a spectrum of artistic renders, visitors will pinpoint the critical balance of qualities to evoke their desired habitat** ❞

Curatorial statement

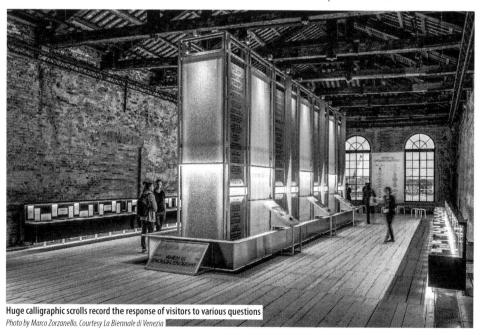

Huge calligraphic scrolls record the response of visitors to various questions
Photo by Marco Zorzanello. Courtesy La Biennale di Venezia

SLOVENIA *(Republic of)*

EXHIBITION TITLE:

+/- 1 °C: In Search of Well-Tempered Architecture

CURATED BY:

Jure Grohar, Eva Gusel, Maša Mertelj, Anja Vidic, Matic Vrabič

EXHIBITORS:

Anna Bach, Eugeni Bach (A&EB architects), Marcello Galiotto, Alessandra Rampazzo (AMAA), Urban Petranovič, Davor Počivašek (Arhitekti Počivašek Petranovič), Niklas Fanelsa (Atelier Fanelsa), Alicja Bielawska, Simone De Iacobis, Aleksandra Kędziorek, Małgorzata Kuciewicz; Laura Bonell, Daniel López-Dòriga (Bonell+Dòriga), Radim Louda, Paul Mouchet (CENTRAL offau), Velika Ivkovska, KOSMOS, Aidas Krutejavq (KSFA Krutejavas Studio For Architecture), Laura Linsi, Roland Reemaa (LLRRLLRR), Benjamin Lafore, Sébastien Martinez-Barat (MBL architectes), Ana Victoria Munteanu, Daniel Tudor Munteanu, Daniel Norell, Einar Rodhe (Norell Rodhe); Søren Pihlmann (Pihlmann architects); Ambra Fabi, Giovanni Piovene (Piovenefabi), Matteo Ghidoni (Salottobuono), Gordon Selbach, Pablo Canga, Anna Herreros (SOLAR), Elena Schütz, Julian Schubert and Leonard Streich (Something Fantastic), Jakob Sellaoui (Studio Jakob Sellaoui), Hana Mohar, Frane Stančić (Studio Ploca), Susanne Brorson (Studio Susanne Brorson), Benjamin Gallegos Gabilondo, Marco Provinciali (Supervoid), Ana Kreč (Svet vmes), Janja Šušnjar, Mireia Luzárraga, Alejandro Muiño (TAKK), Léone Drapeaud, Manuel León Fanjul, Johnny Leya (Traumnovelle), Gaetan Brunet, Chloé Valadié (UR), Javier Garcia-Germán (TAAs)

ARSENALE MAP REF **[A]** P. **15**   *ARSENALE PLAN P. 13*

Venue: Arsenale, Castello

Vaporetto: Arsenale

❯ The curators invited 50 groups of architects from across Europe to suggest one example of vernacular architecture that prioritizes energy efficiency. The Slovenian pavilion discusses five of these, as part of a larger project that also proposes a publication on the subject, and a conference in Ljubljana. The curators believe that architecture's potential lies in changing our perspective rather than just focusing on buildings and materials. They examine how modern structures often separate heating and cooling systems, while vernacular architecture integrated them. The pavilion argues that energy efficiency now focuses on technical and legislative requirements, neglecting the holistic approach of past architecture. It considers the potential for developing energy-efficient residential buildings based on these historical concepts, so that – like our ancestors – we can design houses that are energy-efficient from the start.

➕ COMMISSIONER: Maja Vardjan, Museum of Architecture and Design

VISITING

DATES: 20 May–26 Nov 2023

HOURS: 20 May–30 Sep: Tue, Wed, Thu, Sun 11:00–19:00; Fri, Sat, 11:00–20:00. 1 Oct–26 Nov: Tue–Sun 10:00–18:00. Last entry 15 mins before closing

CLOSED: Mon (except 22 May, 14 Aug, 4 Sep, 16 Oct, 30 Oct, 20 Nov)

ADMISSION: Biennale ticket. Available online only. See p. 9 for full details

TICKET INFO: labiennale. org/en/architecture/2023/ information#tickets

❝ We see this kind of exchange of experiences and networking as a form of a modern global workshop ❞

Curatorial statement

Over 50 groups of architects contribute
Photo by Andrea Avezzù.
Courtesy La Biennale di Venezia

SOUTH AFRICA *(Republic of)*

EXHIBITION TITLE:
The Structure of a People

CURATED BY:
Sechaba Maape, Emmanuel Nkambule, Stephen Steyn

EXHIBITORS:
Zamani Project and Tshwane University of Technology, Mmabe Maila, Kyle Brand, Victor Mokhaba, Tlhologello Sesana, Lethlogonollo, Sesana, Wihan Hendrikz, Luthando Thomas, Kirti Mistry, Carin Smuts, Phadi Mabe, Khalipha Rade, Yamkelwa Sim, Anya Strydom, Jan Truter, Liam Harvey, Tim Presbury, Saskia de Bok, Saleigh Davis, Teegan Isola, Nosipho Ndawonde, Solami Nkabinde, Keyur Moodley, Anna Thomas, Kelly de Gouveia, Rorisang, Monanabela, Tammy Ohlson de Fine, Oratile Mothoagae, Emma Skudde, Priyan Moodley, Michael Peneda, Simphiwe Mlambo, Masego Musi, Sesethu Mbonishweni, Dineo Mogane, Jason du Plessis, Mpinane Qhobela, Nthomeng Matete, Makananelo Maapea, Mapotsane Mohale, Moshebi Mohale, 2BLN, Spies Architects, Breinstorm Brand Architects, Anita Szentesi, Stephen Wessels

ARSENALE   MAP REF **[A]** P. **15**   *ARSENALE PLAN P. 13*

Venue: Arsenale, Castello
Vaporetto: Arsenale

➲ Focuses on the Bokoni civilization, which occupied a vast area, and left behind rock carvings thought to depict building plans. An augmented reality display of a Bokoni homestead ruin allows visitors to experience a digital replica of the original site.

⊕ COMMISSIONER: Ambassador Nosipho Nausca-Jean Jezile

VISITING

DATES: 20 May–26 Nov 2023

HOURS: 20 May–30 Sep: Tue, Wed, Thu, Sun 11:00–19:00; Fri, Sat, 11:00–20:00. 1 Oct–26 Nov: Tue–Sun 10:00–18:00. Last entry 15 mins before closing

CLOSED: Mon (except 22 May, 14 Aug, 4 Sep, 16 Oct, 30 Oct, 20 Nov)

ADMISSION: Biennale ticket. Available online only. See p. 9 for full details

TICKET INFO: labiennale. org/en/architecture/2023/ information#tickets

❝ **We have a key opportunity … to present previously unseen artefacts and thinking that is deeply entrenched in vital Indigenous Knowledge Systems in South Africa** ❞

Curatorial statement

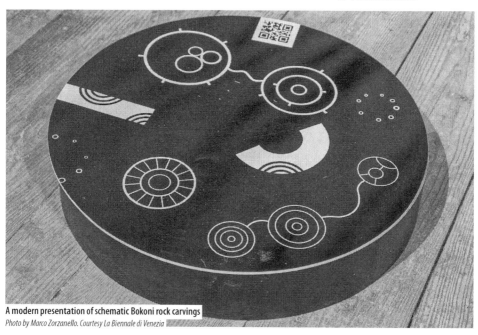

A modern presentation of schematic Bokoni rock carvings
Photo by Marco Zorzanello. Courtesy La Biennale di Venezia

SPAIN

EXHIBITION TITLE:
Foodscapes

CURATED BY:
Eduardo Castillo-Vinuesa, Manuel Ocaña del Valle

EXHIBITORS:
Aldayjover Architecture and Landscape, C+ arquitectas, Common Accounts, Daniel Ibañez + Vicente Guallart+ Manuel Bouzas, Dolores Palacios + Federico Soriano, Elii + María Jerez, Gerard Ortín + Pol Esteve, GRANDEZA + Locument, Guillermo Fernández – Abascal + Urtzi Grau, Institute for Postnatural Studies, Iván L. Munuera + Vivian Rotie + Pablo Saiz, Lucia Jalón Oyarzun, Lucía Tahan, MAIO + Agnes Essonti, Marina Otero Verzier + Manuel Correa, Naranjo-Etxeberría, Pedro Pegenaute

GIARDINI MAP REF **[G]** P. **15**   *GIARDINI PLAN P.* **12**

Venue: Giardini della Biennale, Castello
Vaporetto: Giardini; Giardini Biennale

→ Examines Spain's intersection of agriculture and architecture, via an audiovisual project, a recipe book archive, and public events. The exhibition emphasizes the importance of food in shaping societies and cities, and seeks to envision sustainable models that can feed the world without harming the planet.

foodscapes.es

✚ COMMISSIONER: MITMA (Ministry of Transport, Mobility and Urban Agenda); AECID (Spanish Agency for International Development Cooperation); AC/E (Acción Cultural Española)

VISITING

DATES: 20 May–26 Nov 2023

HOURS: 20 May–30 Sep: Tue–Sun 11:00–19:00. 1 Oct–26 Nov: Tue–Sun 10:00–18:00. Last entry 15 mins before closing

CLOSED: Mon (except 22 May, 14 Aug, 4 Sep, 16 Oct, 30 Oct, 20 Nov)

ADMISSION: Biennale ticket. Available online only. See p. 9 for full details

TICKET INFO: labiennale. org/en/architecture/2023/ information#tickets

❝ **After analysing our food systems … 'Foodscapes' looks to the future to explore other possible models; ones capable of feeding the world without devouring the planet** ❞
Curatorial statement

A metabolic recipe for wine from the exhibition's book archive
Photo by Matteo de Mayda. Courtesy La Biennale di Venezia

SWITZERLAND

EXHIBITION TITLE:
Neighbours

CURATORS / EXHIBITORS:
Karin Sander, Philip Ursprung

GIARDINI   MAP REF **[G]** P. **15**   *GIARDINI PLAN P.* **12**

Venue: Giardini della Biennale, Castello
Vaporetto: Giardini; Giardini Biennale

➲ The Swiss and Venezuelan pavilions are unique in the Giardini because they share a wall. Designed in the 1950s by Bruno Giacometti and Carlo Scarpa respectively, they were built around protected plane trees, resulting in their close proximity. The Swiss curators decided to remove a wall and gates facing the Venezuelan pavilion to transform the architecture into the exhibit itself. By dissolving the borders between the pavilions, they aim to highlight overlooked connections and create a new perspective on their surroundings. The pavilions' architectural and sculptural qualities are emphasized, shifting their purpose from being mere containers to artworks in their own right.

➕ COMMISSIONER: Swiss Arts Council Pro Helvetia: Sandi Paucic, Rachele Giudici Legittimo

VISITING

DATES: 20 May–26 Nov 2023

HOURS: 20 May–30 Sep: Tue–Sun 11:00–19:00. 1 Oct–26 Nov: Tue–Sun 10:00–18:00. Last entry 15 mins before closing

CLOSED: Mon (except 22 May, 14 Aug, 4 Sep, 16 Oct, 30 Oct, 20 Nov)

ADMISSION: Biennale ticket. Available online only. See p. 9 for full details

TICKET INFO: labiennale. org/en/architecture/2023/ information#tickets

❝ **The Swiss and the Venezuelan Pavilions form an ensemble of exceptional architectural and sculptural quality** ❞

Curatorial statement

Giant-size architectural plans of the Swiss and Venezuelan pavilions carpet Switzerland's floor
Photo by Matteo de Mayda. Courtesy La Biennale di Venezia

TÜRKIYE

EXHIBITION TITLE:
Ghost Stories: Carrier Bag Theory of Architecture

CURATED BY:
Sevince Bayrak, Oral Göktaş

PARTICIPANTS:
Various contributors, responding to an open call for suggestions

ARSENALE   MAP REF **[A]** P. **15**   *ARSENALE PLAN P. 13*

Venue: Arsenale, Castello
Vaporetto: Arsenale

➲ The 'Carrier Bag Theory of Evolution', posited by anthropologist Elizabeth Fisher, argues that humans relied on humble carrier bags rather than heroic hunting tools as their first cultural helpers, enabling them to transport gathered vegetables. So instead of focusing on successful or heroic buildings, the exhibition celebrates abandoned structures. The curators collected data on numerous unused buildings, including residences, skyscrapers, schools, and hospitals. They argue that these structures hold the potential to become the 'laboratory of the future' if transformed instead of being destroyed. The urgency to reinforce and repurpose existing buildings has increased after the destructive earthquakes in Kahramanmaraş.

turkiyepavilion23.iksv.org

➕ COMMISSIONER: Istanbul Foundation for Culture and Arts (İKSV)

VISITING

DATES: 20 May–26 Nov 2023

HOURS: 20 May–30 Sep: Tue, Wed, Thu, Sun 11:00–19:00; Fri, Sat, 11:00–20:00. 1 Oct–26 Nov: Tue–Sun 10:00–18:00. Last entry 15 mins before closing

CLOSED: Mon (except 22 May, 14 Aug, 4 Sep, 16 Oct, 30 Oct, 20 Nov)

ADMISSION: Biennale ticket. Available online only. See p. 9 for full details

TICKET INFO: labiennale. org/en/architecture/2023/ information#tickets

❝ Construction becomes an addiction when triggered by economic reasons rather than spatial needs ❞

Curatorial statement

A display of 'expired' Turkish buildings, which the curators suggest could be transformed rather than destroyed

Photo by Marco Zorzanello. Courtesy La Biennale di Venezia

UKRAINE

EXHIBITION TITLE:

Before the Future

CURATED BY:

Iryna Miroshnykova, Oleksii Petrov, Borys Filonenko

PARTICIPANTS:

Nikita Bielokopytov, Daria Borovyk, Oleksandr Burlaka, Alex Bykov, Vadym Denysenko, Oksana Dovgopolova, Nina Dyrenko, Uliana Dzhurliak, Ivan Grabko, Dmytro Gurin, Dana Kosmina, Sasha Kurmaz, Petro Markman, Nataliia Mysak, Anton Oliynyk, Oleksii Pakhomov, Mariia Pakhomova, Ivan Protasov, Daryna Pyrogova, Kateryna Semenyuk, Vadym Sidash, care collective, commercial public art, Prykarpattian Theater, The Center for Spatial Technologies, and others

GIARDINI MAP REF **[G]** P. **15**   *GIARDINI PLAN P.* **12**

Venue: Giardini della Biennale (Central Pavilion), Castello
Vaporetto: Giardini; Giardini Biennale

ARSENALE MAP REF **[A]** P. **15**   *ARSENALE PLAN P.* **13**

Venue: Arsenale, Castello
Vaporetto: Arsenale

> At the Arsenale, a blacked-out room suggests places under siege. Meanwhile the Giardini recreates ancient defensive earthworks near Kyiv that are facing invaders once again.

ukrainianpavilion.org

COMMISSIONER: Mariana Oleskiv, State Agency for Tourism Development of Ukraine

VISITING

DATES: 20 May–26 Nov 2023

GIARDINI HOURS: 20 May–30 Sep: Tue–Sun 11:00–19:00. 1 Oct–26 Nov: Tue–Sun 10:00–18:00. Last entry 15 mins before closing

ARSENALE HOURS: As Giardini, except 20 May–30 Sep there is late opening on Fri and Sat until 20:00

CLOSED: Mon (except 22 May, 14 Aug, 4 Sep, 16 Oct, 30 Oct, 20 Nov)

ADMISSION: Biennale ticket. Available online only. See p. 9 for full details

TICKET INFO: labiennale. org/en/architecture/2023/ information#tickets

66 These spaces, the fortifications, are a place to be quiet, to chill. But it is also a reminder that somewhere, someone is fearing for their safety 99

Borys Filonenko, curator

The Giardini recreates ancient defensive earthworks, intended here as a place to relax
Photo by Matteo de Mayda. Courtesy La Biennale di Venezia

UNITED ARAB EMIRATES

EXHIBITION TITLE:
Aridly Abundant

CURATED BY:
Faysal Tabbarah

ARSENALE MAP REF **[A]** P. **15**   *ARSENALE PLAN P. **13***

Venue: Arsenale, Castello
Vaporetto: Arsenale

➡ This presentation poses the over-arching question: 'What architectural possibilities can emerge when we reimagine arid landscapes as spaces of abundance?'. The display explores the possibilities of using waste materials from UAE's Al Hajar Mountain range in mainstream construction. By scanning and digitizing these materials, the team aims to create new architectural designs. The exhibition reimagines arid landscapes as spaces of abundance, showcasing different aspects of the mountain range's micro-climates. It also looks into historical land-based practices and proposes sharing them with other countries impacted by climate change. It recommends combining historical practices with modern technology for sustainable building in arid environments.

➕ COMMISSIONER: Salama bint Hamdan Al Nahyan Foundation

VISITING

DATES: 20 May–26 Nov 2023

HOURS: 20 May–30 Sep: Tue, Wed, Thu, Sun 11:00–19:00; Fri, Sat, 11:00–20:00. 1 Oct–26 Nov: Tue–Sun 10:00–18:00. Last entry 15 mins before closing

CLOSED: Mon (except 22 May, 14 Aug, 4 Sep, 16 Oct, 30 Oct, 20 Nov)

ADMISSION: Biennale ticket. Available online only. See p. 9 for full details

TICKET INFO: labiennale. org/en/architecture/2023/ information#tickets

❝ **If you integrate land-based practice with technology, you can explore environmentally efficient avenues rooted in the materials and cultural history** ❞

Faysal Tabbarah, curator. Quoted in 'designboom'

Walls combining historical practices with modern technology
Photo by Marco Zorzanello. Courtesy La Biennale di Venezia

UNITED STATES OF AMERICA

EXHIBITION TITLE:
Everlasting Plastics

CURATED BY:
Tizziana Baldenebro, Lauren Leving

EXHIBITORS:
Xavi Laida Aguirre, Simon Anton, Ang Li, Norman Teague, Lauren Yeager

GIARDINI MAP REF **[G]** P. **15**   *GIARDINI PLAN P. 12*

Venue: Giardini della Biennale, Castello
Vaporetto: Giardini; Giardini Biennale

⊙ A colourful yet worrying look at the role of plastic in modern society. Five artists and designers were invited to create works that highlight the material's protean nature. All five consider systems of waste, and their impact on communities – especially in the American Midwest, where the production of petroleum-based polymers is an important part of the industry. The show is being made accessible to US-based audiences with statewide venues, online participation, and workshops that connect Ohio's industries to plastic waste in the Venetian Lagoon.

everlastingplastics.org

⊕ COMMISSIONER: Tizziana Baldenebro, SPACES

VISITING

DATES: 20 May–26 Nov 2023

HOURS: 20 May–30 Sep: Tue–Sun 11:00–19:00. 1 Oct–26 Nov: Tue–Sun 10:00–18:00. Last entry 15 mins before closing

CLOSED: Mon (except 22 May, 14 Aug, 4 Sep, 16 Oct, 30 Oct, 20 Nov)

ADMISSION: Biennale ticket. Available online only. See p. 9 for full details

TICKET INFO: labiennale.org/en/architecture/2023/information#tickets

> ❝ **Plastic is deeply embedded in the culture of the US, where polymers were perfected and exported ... Our toxic chemical relationship with the material is now a global phenomenon** ❞
>
> *Lauren Leving, curator*

Colourful plastic totems in front of the USA pavilion
Photo by Matteo de Mayda. Courtesy La Biennale di Venezia

URUGUAY

EXHIBITION TITLE:

En Ópera. Escenarios futuros de una joven Ley Forestal

CURATED BY:
Mauricio López, Matías Carballal, Andrés Gobba, Sebastián Lambert and Carlos Casacuberta

EXHIBITORS:
INST/MAPA + Carlos Casacuberta, Rafaella Varela, Fol Cvetreznik, Guzmán Bergereau (Exceso Colectivo), Matías Rada, Camila Cardozo (Nomusa), Facundo Balta, Álvaro Silva (AVR), Viki Style (SAK), Noé Núñez Research

GIARDINI   MAP REF **[G]** P. **15**   *GIARDINI PLAN P.* **12**

Venue: Giardini della Biennale, Castello
Vaporetto: Giardini; Giardini Biennale

➲ A dynamic digital opera, with music by young Afro-Uruguayan artists, depicts the impact of the country's Forestry Law of 1987. This complex piece of legislation stated forestry was in the national interest, and has had both positive and negative impacts. The opera reflects on the changes wrought by the law, such as the expansion of monoculture plantations, and the shift from meat to forestry industry exports. A publication provides further context, including an overview of timber construction.

enopera.uy

➕ COMMISSIONER: Facundo de Almeida

VISITING

DATES: 20 May–26 Nov 2023

HOURS: 20 May–30 Sep: Tue–Sun 11:00–19:00. 1 Oct–26 Nov: Tue–Sun 10:00–18:00. Last entry 15 mins before closing

CLOSED: Mon (except 22 May, 14 Aug, 4 Sep, 16 Oct, 30 Oct, 20 Nov)

ADMISSION: Biennale ticket. Available online only. See p. 9 for full details

TICKET INFO: labiennale. org/en/architecture/2023/ information#tickets

❝ **Since the approval of the Forest Law in 1987, the forested surface has grown more than thirty times and this expansion is expected to continue** ❞

Curatorial statement

Visitors watch the immersive digital opera on a giant screen
Photo by Marco Zorzanello. Courtesy La Biennale di Venezia

UZBEKISTAN *(Republic of)*

EXHIBITION TITLE:
Unbuild Together

CURATED BY:
Studio Ko, Karl Fournier & Olivier Marty, Jean-Baptiste Carisé, Sophia Bengebara

EXHIBITORS:
Abdulvokhid Bukhoriy, El Mehdi Azzam, Miza Mucciarelli, Emine Gözde Sevim

ARSENALE   MAP REF **[A]** P. **15**   *ARSENALE PLAN P. **13***

Venue: Arsenale, Castello
Vaporetto: Arsenale

❯ A research project about the ancient Qalas, or fortresses, of Uzbekistan. Qalas are a grand example of the country's rich cultural heritage, and their traditional bricks are fundamental to Uzbek architecture. Such bricks are durable, sustainable, and beautiful, making them suitable for long-lasting building projects. The curators, in collaboration with Ajou University, aim to reinterpret brick making, construction techniques, and surface treatments, resulting in a proposed pavilion design. By studying the Qalas, they hope to learn from the past and make informed design choices for a sustainable future.

➕ COMMISSIONER: Gayane Umerova, Art and Culture Development Foundation

VISITING

DATES: 20 May–26 Nov 2023

HOURS: 20 May–30 Sep: Tue, Wed, Thu, Sun 11:00–19:00; Fri, Sat, 11:00–20:00. 1 Oct–26 Nov: Tue–Sun 10:00–18:00. Last entry 15 mins before closing

CLOSED: Mon (except 22 May, 14 Aug, 4 Sep, 16 Oct, 30 Oct, 20 Nov)

ADMISSION: Biennale ticket. Available online only. See p. 9 for full details

TICKET INFO: labiennale. org/en/architecture/2023/ information#tickets

❝ Our ancient heritage can help us to rethink the trajectory of humanity ❞

Gayane Umerova, Executive Director of the Art and Culture Development Foundation of the Republic of Uzbekistan

High walls evoking Qala fortresses demonstrate the qualities of Uzbek bricks
Photo by Andrea Avezzù. Courtesy La Biennale di Venezia

VENEZUELA
(Bolivarian Republic of)

EXHIBITION TITLE:

Universidad Central de Venezuela, Patrimonio de la Humanidad en recuperación. Ciudad Universitaria de Caracas *(Central University of Venezuela, World Heritage in recovery. University City of Caracas)*

CURATED BY:

Paola Claudia Posani

EXHIBITORS:

Comisión Presidencial para la Recuperación de la UCV

GIARDINI MAP REF **[G]** P. **15**   *GIARDINI PLAN P.* **12**

Venue: Giardini della Biennale, Castello
Vaporetto: Giardini; Giardini Biennale

⊙ A display about the recovery and preservation of the Central University of Venezuela, aka University City of Caracas. Architect Carlos Raúl Villanueva designed and built this masterpiece from 1942 to 1975, and in 2000 it was recognized as a World Heritage Site. Its deteriorating condition led to a significant collapse in 2021, prompting the formation of a commission to protect it. The Venezuelan pavilion itself, by Carlo Scarpa, is another crumbling gem. It shares a party wall with Switzerland, who this year have modified their own pavilion in response to it.

⊕ COMMISSIONER: Paola Claudia Posani

VISITING

DATES: 20 May–26 Nov 2023

HOURS: 20 May–30 Sep: Tue–Sun 11:00–19:00. 1 Oct–26 Nov: Tue–Sun 10:00–18:00. Last entry 15 mins before closing

CLOSED: Mon (except 22 May, 14 Aug, 4 Sep, 16 Oct, 30 Oct, 20 Nov)

ADMISSION: Biennale ticket. Available online only. See p. 9 for full details

TICKET INFO: labiennale. org/en/architecture/2023/ information#tickets

❝ **Villanueva oversaw the campus construction for 20 years ... it remains the only university campus designed by a single architect in the 20th century** ❞

Wikipedia

Documentary displays about University City of Caracas line the elegant Scarpa pavilion
Photo by Marco Zorzanello. Courtesy La Biennale di Venezia

APPLIED ARTS PAVILION

EXHIBITION TITLE:

Tropical Modernism:
Architecture and Power in West Africa

CURATED BY:

Dr Christopher Turner (V&A) with Nana Biamah-Ofosu and Bushra Mohamed (AA)

ARSENALE MAP REF **[A]** P. **15**   *ARSENALE PLAN P. 13*

Venue: Arsenale (Sale d'Armi A), Castello
Vaporetto: Arsenale

❯ Critically examines the history of Tropical Modernism, an architectural style developed in British West Africa. It explores how this style was used to support colonial rule and later adapted by West African architects after Ghana gained independence in 1957. The show focuses on the Department of Tropical Architecture, founded by Maxwell Fry and Jane Drew, and its collaboration with the Kwame Nkrumah University of Science and Technology (KNUST) in Kumasi. It highlights the shift from colonial assumptions to a new architecture that embraced African traditions and a unique local style.

✛ ORGANIZED IN COLLABORATION WITH: The Architectural Association (AA), London, and Kwame Nkrumah University of Science and Technology (KNUST), Kumasi

VISITING

DATES: 20 May–26 Nov 2023

HOURS: 20 May–30 Sep: Tue, Wed, Thu, Sun 11:00–19:00; Fri, Sat, 11:00–20:00. 1 Oct–26 Nov: Tue–Sun 10:00–18:00. Last entry 15 mins before closing

CLOSED: Mon (except 22 May, 14 Aug, 4 Sep, 16 Oct, 30 Oct, 20 Nov)

ADMISSION: Biennale ticket. Available online only. See p. 9 for full details

TICKET INFO: labiennale. org/en/architecture/2023/ information#tickets

  ❝ Tropical Modernism was adapted by Ghanaian architects ... during a transitional moment in which new freedoms were won ❞

Dr Christopher Turner, curator

The images are set on panels inspired by Tropical Modernism tropes
Photo by Andrea Avezzù. Courtesy La Biennale di Venezia

Printing ethical t-shirts at the Top Manta workshop, part of the 'Catelonia in Venice' collateral event

Photo © Eva Serrats, 2023. Courtesy Catalonia in Venice

COLLATERAL EVENTS

An official Biennale strand featuring exhibitions by non-profit institutions

This strand of the official Biennale is for projects by non-profit organizations, ranging from foundations to museums to universities. Also featured are regions not granted National Pavilions, such as Scotland and Catalonia. These events are held all across the city, and are usually free to enter. It's a wide and eclectic array, often in fascinating venues normally closed to the public.

SECTION CONTENTS

A FRAGILE CORRESPONDENCE – SCOTLAND + VENICE

CURATED BY:
Architecture Fringe (Neil McGuire, Andy Summers);
-ism (Alissar Riachi, Aoife Nolan, Amy McEwan, Kristina Enberg);
/other (Mia Pinder-Hussein, Carl C.Z. Jonsson, Alyesha Choudhury)

PARTICIPANTS:
Dr. Amanda Thomson, Raghnaid Sandilands, Hamshya Rajkumar, Dr. Mairi McFadyen, Frank McElhinney, Aaron McCarthy, Prof. Donna Heddle, Dele Adeyemo

CITY MAP REF **[C/1]** P. **14–15**

Venue: Docks Cantieri Cucchini, Fondamenta de Quintavalle, San Pietro di Castello 40
Vaporetto: Giardini; San Pietro di Castello

⊙ This project focuses on three distinct Scottish landscapes – the Highlands, Islands, and Lowlands – via the forests around Loch Ness, the seashore of the Orkney archipelago, and the industrial remnants of Ravenscraig steelworks. Writers, artists, and architects address the local issues deeply rooted in these landscapes, and make clear their global relevance.
scotlandandvenice.com/project/a-fragile-correspondence

⊕ ORGANIZING INSTITUTION: Scotland + Venice

VISITING

DATES: 20 May–26 Nov 2023
HOURS: 20 May–30 Sep: Tue–Sun 11:00–19:00. 1 Oct–26 Nov: Tue–Sun 10:00–18:00
CLOSED: Mon (except 22 May, 14 Aug, 4 Sep, 16 Oct, 30 Oct, 20 Nov)
ADMISSION: Free

❝ Our landscapes are constantly transmitting information if we choose to see and listen ❞
Curatorial statement

Rear view of the pavilion, situated in the picturesque Cantieri Cucchini docks
Photo by Daniele Sambo. Courtesy Creative Scotland

Birch trees by Hamshya Rajkumar in the 'Ravenscraig' section of the exhibition
Photo by Daniele Sambo. Courtesy Creative Scotland

CATALONIA IN VENICE_
FOLLOWING THE FISH

CURATED BY:

Leve Productora
(Daniel Cid, Eva Serrats, Francesc Pla)

PARTICIPANTS:
Top Manta

CITY   MAP REF **[C/2]**   P. **14–15**

Venue: Docks Cantieri Cucchini, Fondamenta de Quintavalle,
San Pietro di Castello 40/A
Vaporetto: Giardini; San Pietro di Castello

➡ Top Manta is a cooperative of Barcelona street vendors from
Senegal, who earn a living selling goods laid out on blankets
– known as 'mantas' – on city streets. They formed the People's
Union of Street Vendors in 2015 and established Top Manta
in 2017, creating ethical fashion and acting as a voice for the
dispossessed. This installation transforms the old docks into
a quasi-street market, with 'mantas' that would normally hold
items for sale instead displaying items relating to the migrants'
journeys. The title parallels these with the large-scale removal
of fish from West African coasts, to feed salmon in northern fish
farms – thus causing African fishing communities to migrate.

fish.llull.cat

➕ ORGANIZING INSTITUTION: Institut Ramon Lull

VISITING

DATES: 20 May–26 Nov 2023

HOURS: 20 May–30 Sep: Tue–
Sun 11:00–19:00. 1 Oct–26 Nov:
Tue–Sun 10:00–18:00

CLOSED: Mon (except 22 May, 14
Aug, 4 Sep, 16 Oct, 30 Oct, 20 Nov)

ADMISSION: Free

❝ **Despite their
difficult living
conditions, migrant
communities develop
creative approaches
and alternative
politics in their
places of arrival** ❞

Curatorial statement

Top Manta worker with posters of the 'manteros' struggles in the background
Photo © Eva Serrats, 2023. Courtesy Catalonia in Venice

CLIMATE WUNDERKAMMER

CURATED BY:

Ceren Sezer, Christa Reicher, Eugenio Morello, Francesco Musco

PARTICIPATING UNIVERSITIES:

Alexandria University, Chalmers University of Technology, Delft University of Technology, German Jordanian University, International Union of Architects, IUAV University of Venice, Politecnico di Milano, RWTH Aachen University, Singapore University of Technology and Design, University of Pretoria

PARTICIPANTS INCLUDE:

Andy van den Dobbelsteen, Carlo Federico dall'Omo, Cem Ataman, Chrisna du Plessis, Daniele Santucci, International Union of Architects, Israa Mahmoud, Jan Hugo, Liane Thuvander, Maram Tawil, Mohamed Assem Hanafy, Monica Billger, Vittorio Negretto

CITY   MAP REF **[C/3]** P. **14–15**

Venue: IUAV Palazzo Badoer (ground floor), Calle de la Laca, San Polo 2468
Vaporetto: Piazzale Roma; San Tomà

➲ A multi-media presentation by young students who see how rapidly climate change is impacting our planet. Includes an installation of bottles containing messages on the theme, plus projections, sounds, and an interactive table with a world map illustrating climate hazards and practical solutions.

climatewunderkammer.org

✚ ORGANIZING INSTITUTION: RWTH Aachen University

VISITING

DATES: 20 May–26 Nov 2023
HOURS: Mon–Fri 10:00–18:00
CLOSED: Sat–Sun and Jun 2, Aug 14–18, Nov 1, Nov 20–21
ADMISSION: Free

❝ **Young generations can help us make the 'invisible visible' by comparing before and after the climate event hit our regions, communities, and places** ❞
Curatorial statement

Promotional image for the event
Courtesy Climate Wunderkammer

DIACHRONIC APPARATUSES OF TAIWAN. *Architecture as on-going details within landscape*

CURATED BY:
Wei Tseng with co-curators Jeong-Der Ho,
Meng-Tsung Su, Sheng-Chieh Ko (from the
Architectural Department of Tunghai University)

PARTICIPATING UNIVERSITIES:
**Chung Yuan Christian University, Feng Chia University,
National Cheng Kung University, Tamkang University, Tunghai University**

CITY   MAP REF **[C/4]** P. **14–15**

Venue: Palazzo delle Prigioni, Riva degli Schiavoni, Castello 4209
Vaporetto: San Marco Giardinetti; San Marco Vallaresso; San Zaccaria

➲ This exhibition explores how people in Taiwan have historically shaped diverse architectural forms in agricultural landscapes across different altitudes and latitudes. It highlights the country's unique climate variations, from cold zone highlands to tropical lowlands, which support a rich biodiversity. The objective is to initiate a dialogue between synthetic and natural environments and to learn from the countryside. The curators have taken a school-centric approach, involving teachers and students from several faculties.

ntmofa.gov.tw

➕ ORGANIZING INSTITUTION: National Taiwan Museum of Fine Arts

VISITING

DATES: 20 May–26 Nov 2023
HOURS: Tue–Sun 10:00–18:00
CLOSED: Mon
ADMISSION: Free

❝ **The main purpose of this exhibition is to promote the dialogue between the built landscape and the real land: people have been in awe of the land from the primitive period** ❞
Curatorial statement

Simulation photo of the Taiwan collateral event at Palazzo delle Prigioni
Courtesy Department of Architecture, Tunghai University

EUMIES AWARDS. *Young Talent 2023. The Laboratory of Education*

JURY:

Jennifer Mack (Associate Professor and Docent at KTH Stockholm);
Manuel Henriques (Executive Director at the Lisbon Architecture Triennale);
N'Goné Fall (independent curator and cultural policies specialist);
Simone Sfriso (Co-founder of TAMassociati); Snežana Vesnić (Assistant
Professor at the University of Belgrade – Faculty of Architecture)

YOUNG TALENT FINALISTS:

**Anthony Keniry, James Stack; Charline van Maercke; Dimitrios Mitsimponas;
Dinko Jelecevic; Jaakko Torvinen, Elli Wendelin nee Hirvonen; Laura Hurley;
Lenart Piano; María de la O Molina Pérez-Tomé; Merilin Kaup; Merve Sahin;
Patricia Nieto Pujadas; Xenia Stoumpou, Valerian Andonis Portokalis**

YOUNG TALENT OPEN FINALISTS:

Katya Krat; Mia Pulles; Ruta Perminaite; Shaha Raphael; Tiia Partanen

CITY MAP REF **[C/5]** P. **14–15**

Venue: Palazzo Mora, Strada Nova, Cannaregio 3659
Vaporetto: Ca' d'Oro

→ Supports recently graduated architects, urban planners, and
landscape architects in Europe, with selected works published
online and in a booklet. Winners have the chance to collaborate
and learn from established firms and institutions of their choice.
Also includes the Young Talent Open, for schools from Africa
and non-Creative Europe members of the Council of Europe.
eumiesawards.com

⊕ ORGANIZING INSTITUTION: Fundació Mies van der Rohe

VISITING

DATES: 20 May–26 Nov 2023
HOURS: Wed–Mon 10:00–18:00
CLOSED: Tue
ADMISSION: Free

❝ **The award has helped the winners from the previous editions to set out their careers in consolidated architecture offices, set up their own practices, and share their knowledge in universities** ❞

Curatorial statement

The awards support a range of disciplines
Courtesy YTAA

RADICAL YET POSSIBLE FUTURE SPACE SOLUTIONS

CURATED BY:

Francesca Bria, John Schellnhuber, Wael Al Awar

DAY 1:

Activation of collective thinking

PARTICIPANTS INCLUDE:

Alexandra Mitsotaki, Aric Chen, Benedetta Tagliabue, Christoph de Jaeger, Clara Latini, Edgar Pieterse, Elisa Zatta , Eszter Dàvida, Eva Franch I Gilabert, Federica Rossi , Francesco Bergamo , Gerfried Stocker, Giulia Foscari, Hilda Flavia Nakabuye, Hubert Trammer, Jacopo Galli , John Schellnhuber , Jose Luis de Vincente, José Pedro Sousa, Kunle Adyani, Lorenza Baroncelli, Luther Quenum, Markus Reymann, Mattia Bertin , Michael Gorman, Michela Magas, Michela Pace , Orla Murphy, Petr Skvaril, Pia Maier Schriever, Prodomos Tsiavos, Rem Koolhaas, Sheela Patel, Shigeru Ban, Stefano Mancuso, Stephan Petermann, Thiemo Heilbron, Wael Al Awar, Xu Tiantian

CITY MAP REF **[C/6]** P. **14–15**

Venue: IUAV Ca' Tron, Calle Tron, Santa Croce 1957
Vaporetto: Rialto Mercato; Riva de Biasio

DAY 2:

From collective thinking to creative disputes

PARTICIPANTS INCLUDE:

Aric Chen, Benno Albrecht, Carlo Barbante, Clara Latini, Edgar Peterse, Gerfried Stocker, Giulia Foscari, Jose Luis de Vincente, Jose Pedro Sousa, Markus Reymann, Michael Gorman, Orla Murphy, Pia Maier Schriever, Sheela Patel, Xu Tiantian; Guest speakers: Benno Albrecht, Elisa Ferreira, Lesley Lokko, Luigi Brugnaro, Ursula Von der Leyen

CITY MAP REF **[C/7]** P. 14–15

Venue: IUAV Tolentini (in Aula Magna), off Fondamenta dei Tolentini, Santa Croce 191
Vaporetto: Piazzale Roma

○ Through its creative initiative The New European Bauhaus, the European Union presents its first event at the International Architecture Exhibition. The packed two-day session features influential speakers such as Ursula von der Leyen, President of the European Commission, and renowned architects Rem Koolhaas and Shigeru Ban. Curated by experts in innovation, physics, and architecture, the event focuses on exploring radical yet feasible actions to better utilize space and resources. The participants discuss new ways of living and challenge the notion that future solutions are limited to existing ones. The conference includes masterclasses, parallel discussions, and interdisciplinary debates aimed at finding collective sustainable solutions for the future.

new-european-bauhaus.europa.eu/radical-yet-possible-future-space-solutions_en

⊕ ORGANIZING INSTITUTION: New European Bauhaus, Joint Research Centre of the European Commission

VISITING

Day 1

DATE: 25 May 2023

HOURS: Thu 15:00–18:00

ADMISSION: Free. Students only. Registration now closed

VISITING TIP: The entrance is at the end of Calle Tron, beyond which is a big hidden complex.

Day 2

DATE: 26 May 2023

HOURS: Fri 11:00–17:30

ADMISSION: Free. Open access. Registration now closed

VISITING TIP: Aula Magna means great hall. Also note the famous Carla Scarpa main entrance to the entire complex.

VIEW AT: There is a livestream of day two on YouTube. The link is: *youtube.com/watch?v=IJ0gEcpF8cs*

❝ **The New European Bauhaus is a think-do tank. A design lab, accelerator and network at the same time ... at the crossroads between art, culture and science** ❞

Curatorial statement

STUDENTS AS RESEARCHERS: *Creative Practice and University Education*

CURATED BY:

Maria Perbellini

STUDENTS/RESEARCHERS:
Students from invited architecture schools around the world

CITY   MAP REF **[C/8]** P. **14–15**

Venue: Centro Studi e Documentazione della Cultura Armena, Calle Zappa Dorsoduro, Dorsoduro 1602 (entrance from Corte Zappa)
Vaporetto: San Basilio

○ Highlights the transformative potential of university education in challenging market-oriented societies. It emphasizes the role of students in driving an environmental revolution while ensuring the well-being of future generations. The exhibition features proposals and projects by architecture students from around the world, under the umbrella title 'Global Mass – Living Mass. Beyond Artificiality: Living Materials'. Its physical element, 'University Dialogs', is a multi-media installation that records and recomposes this collective creative effort. A companion virtual exhibition, titled 'Knowledge Transfer', expands on its themes to connect research, design, and practice.

⊕ ORGANIZING INSTITUTION: New York Institute of Technology

VISITING

DATES: 20 May–26 Nov 2023
HOURS: 20 May–30 Sep: Tue–Sun 11:00–19:00. 1 Oct–26 Nov: Tue–Sun 10:00–18:00
CLOSED: Mon (except 22 May, 14 Aug, 4 Sep, 16 Oct, 30 Oct, 20 Nov)
ADMISSION: Free

❝ **University education represents an opportunity to develop radical visions that can challenge the conventionality of market-oriented societies** ❞

Curatorial statement

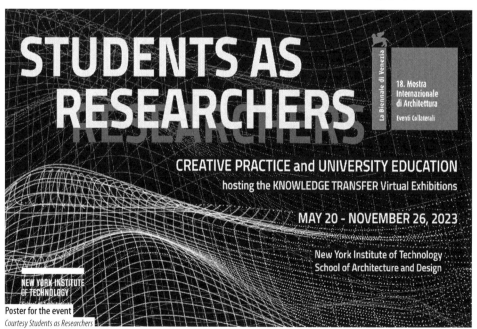

Poster for the event
Courtesy Students as Researchers

TRACÉ BLEU. *Que faire en ce lieu, à moins que l'on y songe?*

CURATED BY:
Architecturestudio, Centquatre-Paris

PARTICIPANTS:
Krijn de Koning, Joanie Lemercier, Jonathas de Andrade, Serge Bloch

CITY MAP REF **[C/9]** P. **14–15**

Venue: Campiello Santa Maria Nova, Cannaregio 6024
Vaporetto: Fondamenta Nove; Rialto

➲ The curators present their book 'Tracé Bleu' alongside an exhibition of the same name. The book shares their ideas on reorienting the care of inhabited environments for the next 50 years, in response to the new climate regime. The exhibition expands on these ideas via the imaginations of four artists, also taking into consideration the Biennale's theme of 'The Laboratory of the Future'. The theatrical setting encourages dialogue and debate, transforming individual knowledge into creative potential. The exhibition's title – in English, 'Blue Trace: what to do in this place unless we think about it?' – reflects its theme. The host venue, CA' ASI, is a cultural venue created by Architecturestudio in 2009, conceived as a think tank for urban, architectural and artistic reflections.

➕ ORGANIZING INSTITUTION: CA' ASI

VISITING

DATES: 20 May–26 Nov 2023
HOURS: Wed–Sun 11:00–18.30
CLOSED: Mon–Tue
ADMISSION: Free

❝ From the very beginning, the practice has believed in the virtues of exchange, crossing ideas, common effort, shared knowledge and enthusiasm ❞

Architecturestudio, curator

The exterior of the venue announces the exhibition's presence
Courtesy Architecturestudio

TRANSFORMATIVE HONG KONG

CURATED BY:

Hendrik Tieben, Sarah Lee, Yutaka Yano

PARTICIPANTS:

Arup, Building Narrative with Kris Provoost Photography, CUHK Research Lab, HIR Studio, Hiroyuki Shinohara and Tung Hoi, Peter Chan, Justin Hui, Lead8, Rocco Design Architects Associates Ltd, Studio RYTE, The MTR Corporation, Tobias Klein and Pok Yin Victor Leung

CITY MAP REF **[C/10]** P. **14–15**

Venue: Ramo de la Tana, off Campo de la Tana (opposite Arsenale entrance), Castello 2126
Vaporetto: Arsenale

➲ Explores several transformational Hong Kong projects, from the macro to the micro. Topics range from Hong Kong's climate action plan to advancements in 3D printed ceramics. Projects include the Northern Link transport system, intended to provide accessible and eco-friendly mobility to the northern New Territories; the East Kowloon Cultural Centre, which combines housing and cultural needs; and a deep dive (not literally) into the redevelopment of Victoria Harbour.

2023.vbexhibitions.hk

➕ ORGANIZING INSTITUTION: Hong Kong Arts Development Council + Hong Kong Institute of Architects Biennale Foundation

VISITING

DATES: 20 May–26 Nov 2023
HOURS: 20 May–30 Sep: Tue–Sun 11:00–19:00. 1 Oct–26 Nov: Tue–Sun 10:00–18:00
CLOSED: Mon (except 22 May, 14 Aug, 4 Sep, 16 Oct, 30 Oct, 20 Nov)
ADMISSION: Free

❝ **The exhibition introduces a unique insight into selected critical urban issues facing Hong Kong in the near future** ❞

Professor Hendrik Tieben, curator

A mockup of the exhibition, showing the exterior courtyard from above
Image courtesy Transformative Hong Kong exhibition

INDEX

A quick way to find anything in this book

Includes all the exhibitions in alphabetical
order with their page numbers; and all the
venue addresses, with an explanation of the
idiosyncratic Venetian street numbering system

A–Z INDEX OF EXHIBITIONS

An alphabetical list of all the exhibitions, followed by their page numbers

A–Z INDEX OF ADDRESSES

An alphabetical list of all the venues, with their addresses and exhibitions

Address	Exhibition
Abbazia di San Giorgio Maggiore Isola di San Giorgio Maggiore	*Holy See*
Arsenale Ramo de la Tana (off Campo de la Tana), Castello	*Biennale main site*
Associazione Culturale Spiazzi Fondamenta del Pistor (off Ponte Storto), Castello 3865	*Cyprus*
Associazione Vela al Terzo Venezia Fondamenta Calle Giazzo, Castello 209	*Grenada*
Calle San Lorenzo Castello 5063/B	*San Marino*
Campiello Santa Maria Nova Cannaregio 6024	*Tracé Bleu. Que faire en ce lieu, à moins que l'on y songe?*
Campo della Tana Castello 2125 (entrance in Ramo della Tana)	*Lithuania*
Castello 96 Salizada Streta (at base of ramp to Giardino delle Vergini), Castello 96	*Estonia*
Centro Culturale don Orione Artigianelli Zattere, Dorsoduro 919	*Bulgaria*
Centro Studi e Documentazione della Cultura Armena Calle Zappa Dorsoduro (entrance from Corte Zappa), Dorsoduro 1602	*Students as Researchers*
Docks Cantieri Cucchini 40 Fondamenta de Quintavalle, San Pietro di Castello 40	*A Fragile Correspondence – Scotland + Venice*

THE VENICE ADDRESS SYSTEM

Venice is divided into six 'sestiere', or districts: San Marco, San Polo, Santa Croce, Cannaregio, Castello, and Dorsoduro. Each has its own number sequence, with Santa Croce 55 being the building in Santa Croce numbered 55, and San Marco 55 the one in San Marco numbered 55. Islands have their own individual sequences, such as Giudecca 43 or San Pietro di Castello 40. Multiple-occupancy sites include letters, such as Dorsoduro 919/A. These numbers are displayed outside each address, usually painted on the wall, and proceed – like the streets – in a labyrinthine manner. Road names are generally added before the sestiere, to give a better idea of location; however landmarks such as churches and palazzi do not always include streets or numbers as part of their official address. Note that some street names, such as Calle del Forno, occur more than once, and online maps (not always accurate for Venice) may choose the wrong one. So it is wise to check the sestiere name as well, to ensure it is in the correct part of the island.

Address	Exhibition
Docks Cantieri Cucchini 40/A Fondamenta de Quintavalle, San Pietro di Castello 40/A	*Catalonia in Venice_* *Following the Fish*
Forte Marghera Via Forte Marghera 30, Mestre, Venice 30173	*The Laboratory of the Future* *(Sweet Water offsite project)*
Giardini della Biennale Viale Trento, Castello	*Biennale main site*
Il Giardino Bianco Art Space Via Giuseppe Garibaldi, Castello 1814	*Georgia*
IUAV Ca' Tron Calle Tron, Santa Croce 1957	*Radical yet possible future* *space solutions (25 May)*
IUAV Palazzo Badoer Calle de la Laca, San Polo 2468	*Climate Wunderkammer*
IUAV Tolentini Off Fondamenta dei Tolentini, Santa Croce 191	*Radical yet possible future* *space solutions (26 May)*
Magazzino del Sale 5 Fondamenta Zattere ai Saloni, Dorsoduro 262	*Kuwait*
New Gallery of the Romanian Institute for Culture and Humanistic Research (aka Istituto Romeno di Cultura e Ricerca Umanistica), Palazzo Correr, Campo Santa Fosca, Cannaregio 2214	*Romania (also in Giardini)*
Palazzo delle Prigioni Riva degli Schiavoni, Castello 4209	*Diachronic Apparatuses* *of Taiwan*
Palazzo Franchetti Campiello San Vidal, San Marco 2847	*Portugal*
Palazzo Malipiero Ramo Malipiero (off Campo San Samuele), San Marco 3078–3079/A	*Montenegro*
Palazzo Mora Strada Nova, Cannaregio 3659	*EUmies Awards.* *Young Talent 2023*
Ramo de la Tana Off Campo de la Tana (opposite Arsenale entrance), Castello 2126	*Transformative Hong Kong*
San Servolo Isola di San Servolo	*Niger*
Scuola dei Laneri Salizada San Pantalon, Santa Croce 131/A	*North Macedonia*
Tana Art Space Fondamenta de la Tana, Castello 2109/A and 2110–2111	*Panama*

CREDITS AND ATTRIBUTIONS

Original content

All original text, maps, and graphic design by and © Vici MacDonald, 2023.

Official statements

Any texts described as 'from the official statement' are extracts from the official publicity material supplied for press use and listings, lightly edited for length and clarity only.

Third-party quotes

Third-party quotes have attributions and sources beneath them. Where they are credited as 'Curatorial statement', the quote is from the official publicity material, as above.

Original photos

All original photos in this book are by and © Vici MacDonald.

Publicity photos

All other photos are either official publicity shots supplied for press use and listings, or from Wikimedia Commons. All sources are credited below the caption.

The Giardini's Sant'Elena exit
Photo © Vici MacDonald

NOTES

Space for your own
jottings and visuals

NOTES

NOTES

NOTES

Printed in Germany
by Amazon Distribution
GmbH, Leipzig